Edwin Gilpin

The Mines and Mineral Lands of Nova Scotia

Edwin Gilpin

The Mines and Mineral Lands of Nova Scotia

ISBN/EAN: 9783743324862

Manufactured in Europe, USA, Canada, Australia, Japa

Cover: Foto ©ninafisch / pixelio.de

Manufactured and distributed by brebook publishing software (www.brebook.com)

Edwin Gilpin

The Mines and Mineral Lands of Nova Scotia

THE
Mines and Mineral Lands
OF
NOVA SCOTIA.

BY

EDWIN GILPIN, Jr., A.M., F. G. S.,

INSPECTOR OF MINES FOR THE PROVINCE OF NOVA SCOTIA,
MEMBER OF THE N. OF E. INSTITUTE OF M. AND M. E., ETC.,

HALIFAX, N. S.:
ROBERT T. MURRAY, QUEEN'S PRINTER.
1880.

HALIFAX, N. S.,
March 31, 1880.

The Hon. S. H. HOLMES,
Provincial Secretary:

SIR,—I beg leave to submit the following report on the Mines and Mineral Lands of Nova Scotia. In it I have endeavored to give, without entering into mineralogical details, such information as will convey a correct idea of the Minerals found in the Province, their distribution, etc., and have referred to the probability of their number being increased by future discoveries.

I have the honor to remain,
Your obedient servant,
EDWIN GILPIN, JR.,
Inspector of Mines.

CONTENTS.

INTRODUCTION.
GENERAL REMARKS.—GEOLOGY OF NOVA SCOTIA.

CHAPTER I.

Page.

Coal—Shales—Petroleum... 1

CHAPTER II.
METALS AND THEIR ORES.

Gold... 30
Iron... 51
Copper... 74
Lead and Silver.. 82
Antimony—Molybdenum—Nickel and Cobalt—Zinc—Tin.............. 85

CHAPTER III.
MINERALS APPLICABLE TO CERTAIN CHEMICAL MANUFACTURES.

Sulphur and Arsenic Ores—Celestine—Manganese..................... 89

CHAPTER IV.
MINERAL MANURES.

Gypsum—Phosphates... 93

CHAPTER V.
MINERAL PIGMENTS.

Barytes—Ochres.. 97

CHAPTER VI.

Salt—Mineral Waters... 100

CHAPTER VII.
MINERALS APPLICABLE TO BUILDING PURPOSES.

Freestone—Granite—Flags and Slates—Clay—Limestones—Marbles—Cements.. 104

CHAPTER VIII.

REFRACTORY MINERALS.

Page.

Plumbago—Fire Clay—Soapstone—Pottery Clay—Kaolin..............111

CHAPTER IX.

MATERIALS FOR GRINDING AND POLISHING.

Infusorial Earth—Grindstones—Millstones—Whetstones..............115

CHAPTER X.

Precious Stones—Trap Minerals....................................117

CHAPTER XI.

Minerals of the Laurentian Strata—Tenure of Mineral Lands—United States Tariff..119

APPENDIX.

Coal Sales in Nova Scotia, 1875 to 1879.
Coal Exported to the United States.
Coal Trade by Counties.
Coal Produce year 1879.
Colliery Labor Returns.
Gold, General Annual Summary.
Gold, District Summary.

INTRODUCTION.

In the following pages I have endeavored to describe, as concisely as possible, the mineral resources of Nova Scotia.

It will be seen that this Province holds in juxtaposition coal, iron and gold—a boon nature has conferred on few countries. The importance of this appears more fully when it is remembered that no other Province of the Dominion is similarly favored. The development of our iron ores and coal must form an important page in our future history. Indications of the presence of valuable ores of copper have been discovered, although as yet they are almost untested. Among the minerals that have been worked and present themselves over large tracts of country, permitting a greatly increased out-put, may be mentioned the ores of Manganese, Gypsum, and Barytes; Ochres, Brine, Marble, etc.

Our deposits of what may be termed domestic minerals, such as Gypsum, Limestone, Building-stones, Clays, etc., are of unlimited extent, and good quality.

In the absence of geological surveys, embracing the whole of the Province, it would be premature to venture beyond a bare reference to the districts likely to contain valuable minerals. It may, however, be remarked that I am able to give, from authentic sources, the extent of our coal fields. The area of the gold districts has been estimated at about 3,000 square miles. The iron ores of the Province are as yet known only in isolated localities, the total extent of which can hardly be estimated. When, however, it is considered that the ore properties of the only two companies who have turned their attention to the subject cover 55 and 30 square miles, without monopolising their respective districts, the extent of the deposits will be understood. There being comparatively no demand for iron ores, but little search has been made; should enquiries be raised, doubtless many new deposits would be found.

The occurrence of "Laurentian" strata in the Province leads to the hope that the valuable minerals characterising them in Ontario and Quebec may be found here also.

The information that I have been able to collect will show that we possess the materials required for building up large mining and manufacturing industries. As this knowledge gains ground, capitalists and practical men will perceive the advantages offered to the miner by the Nova Scotia Government, and the natural assistance afforded by our position as the nearest of England's colonies and the future manufacturing Province of the Dominion.

In this Union the position to be assumed by Nova Scotia is apparently that of the workshop, in which our own and imported raw materials may be elaborated for the agricultural lands of the West, which will send us food in return for the products of our labor.

GEOLOGY OF NOVA SCOTIA.

I give the following outline of the Geology of Nova Scotia, as serving to indicate, in a rough manner, the extent and ages of the strata, which at one point present to the farmer soils well adapted to recompense his labors, and at another hold the treasures which excite the cupidity of the miner.

The valley of the Annapolis River and the north shore of the Basin of Minas are occupied by measures of the Triassic age. They are not known to contain any minerals of economic value, and are interesting chiefly in connection with the trap-dykes which form a prominent feature in the Bay of Fundy landscape, and contain many curious and beautiful minerals.

The Carboniferous measures next claim attention. These strata are subdivided, by Dr. Dawson and others, into five groups.

1st. The Upper Coal Measures, composed of red and gray sandstones, marls and shales. In this series coal seams are frequently met, as at Merigomish, Pictou, Wallace, etc., not however, large enough to allow profitable workings to be carried on. The Upper Coal Measures are met in the centre of the Cumberland coal field, in Colchester and in Pictou Counties.

2nd. The True Coal Measures. These strata contain all the workable seams at present known in this Province, and have been carefully surveyed by the officers of the Dominion Geological Survey. They are met in Cumberland, Pictou, Antigonish, Cape Breton, Richmond, Victoria and Inverness Counties. Outliers of those strata are believed to exist in Kings, Digby and Hants Counties, but their age has not yet been settled. The thickness of this formation has been considered by Dr. Dawson to average 4,000 feet.

3rd. The Millstone Grit occurs at the base of the coal measures, and is particularly developed in Cumberland and Cape Breton Counties. It yields in the former county valuable beds of grindstones, etc., but nowhere, so far as I am aware, does it contain any seams of coal.

4th. The Lower Carboniferous Marine Formation. This is one of the most valuable of the rocks series found in the Province. Its detrition furnishes an excellent soil, and the beds of limestone and gypsum which abound in it provide unlimited supplies of two indispensible minerals. It occupies large tracts in Hants and Colchester Counties, and is extensively developed in Cumberland, Pictou, Antigonish and Kings Counties, and in all parts of Cape Breton. The greater portion of the best farming land of the Province is underlaid by this set of rocks.

5th. The Lower Coal Measures. These strata are met at Horton, and in Hants and Cape Breton Counties. They are distinguished by an abundance of black bituminous and carbonaceous shales, so that they are often considered to be coal-bearing. As yet, however, no workable coal beds have been found in them.

The extent of the carboniferous measures in Nova Scotia may be estimated at 5,000 square miles. As yet the various subdivisions have not all been mapped out, attention having hitherto been directed to the coal-producing districts.

Devonian.—The iron ore bearing strata, of the south side of the Annapolis Valley, have been described by Dr. Dawson as Devonian, but his conclusions are disputed by Dr. Honeyman, the Provincial Geologist, who is inclined to consider them of much greater age. The labors of the Geological Survey have indicated extensive areas in Richmond and Cape Breton Counties, as being probably Devonian, but this opinion may be modified on more extended surveys. These strata, as met in Annapolis County, contain very valuable beds of magnetic and hematite iron ores, which are known to extend over a considerable range of country.

Upper Silurian.—Our knowledge of the extent of these measures is not yet complete. In this connection Dr. Honeyman has rendered valuable service by his labors at Arisaig. From this point, which may be considered the key of the Silurian geology of Nova Scotia, he has traced them through Pictou, Cumberland and Kings Counties. These strata hold valuable deposits of bedded iron ores, and are in this respect typically developed in Pictou County.

Lower Silurian.—These measures occupy large districts at several points in Cape Breton and Nova Scotia, but no systematic surveys have as yet defined their limits. Succeeding these strata come a vast area of strata considered to embrace all the older measures typically developed in Canada proper.

The labors of Dr. Honeyman, and of Mr. H. Fletcher, of the Geological Survey, have shown large areas of Laurentian strata, with limestones and iron ores similar to those characterising the Laurentian of Ontario and Quebec.

The age of the strata holding the gold-bearing lodes of the Atlantic coast has not yet been settled. Including their associated granites, they are estimated to cover 7,500 square miles of the Province. The remaining 6,000 square miles are considered as occupied by Silurian and Devonian and Triassic Strata.

Dr. Dawson's classical work on Acadian Geology gives full details of the distribution of the various rock systems. The proceedings of the Nova Scotia Institute of Natural Science contain many valuable papers by Dr. Honeyman, illustrating the extent and divisions of the Silurian system. The reports of the Canadian Geological Survey since the year 1869 contain valuable reports on our coal and iron fields, as well as on the structural geology of Cape Breton.

From the above works a correct idea can be gathered of Nova Scotia geology, as worked out up to the present date chiefly by the labors of unaided individuals. When it is considered how little really is known of the ages, distribution and economic values of our pre-carboniferous strata, the importance and even necessity of a complete survey of the Province becomes apparent. Further allusions to this will be found in this report, but it may be remarked that the direct benefits accruing from such a survey would many times outweigh the expense of its execution.

THE MINES AND MINERAL LANDS

OF NOVA SCOTIA.

CHAPTER I.

COAL.—SHALES.—PETROLEUM.

The Coal Fields of Nova Scotia.—The history of our coal trade is so admirably treated by Mr. Richard Brown, that I need not recapitulate facts within the memory of most people; but may proceed at once to lay before you all the information that I have been able to collect bearing on the extent of our coal deposits, the nature of the seams, and the uses to which they are applicable.

Nova Scotia Coal belongs entirely to the bituminous division of Dana, no anthracite having been met as yet. It may be subdivided into coking, cherry or free-burning, and cannel coal.

In the following description the various coal-producing districts will be arranged in order from the eastern extremity of the Province—the thickness of the beds, their composition, names of chief mines, and other information being submitted.

It may be premised that the productive coal measures of Nova Scotia belong to the same horizon in the Geological sequence as those of England and the United States, and present many points of intimate connection in fossil remains, and in the associated strata. Dr. Dawson's "Acadian Geology" gives very full accounts of the mode of formation, and of the flora of our coal measures, any notice of which would, although very interesting, be foreign to the scope of this report.

CAPE BRETON

Sydney Coal Field.—This district occupies the north-east corner of Cape Breton, and a small portion of Victoria, Counties. Mr. Robb, in his reports (Geo. Sur. 1872-3), estimates the extent of the coal district at 200 square miles, its dimensions being about 32 miles from the north-west to south-east, and 6 in width. This coal field forms the area of an extensive basin, the greater part of which is hidden beneath the Atlantic. Fortunately, however, nearly all of the seams can be followed in their subaqueous extension, and rights have been taken out covering about 100 square miles of the sub-marine coal.

Mr. Poole, in his report to the Commissioner of Mines for the year 1877, says:

"Assuming for the present a contour line three miles from shore to be the boundary of profitable working, and four thousand feet the available depth, and that no seam under three feet will be worked, then taking into consideration the minimum cover of solid measures required by our present law, the reduction to be made on account of known anticlinals, and the average thickness of the seams along their shore crops, the sub-marine coal field of Cape Breton, from Mira Bay to Cape Dauphin, will yield 1,866,000,000 tons. This estimate assumes that after allowing one fourteenth for unavoidable loss and waste in working, 1,400 tons may be obtained from each foot acre, as was assumed in the enquiry by the Royal Commission to ascertain the quantity of coal remaining unwrought in Great Britain."

The estimates of Mr. Brown and others make the total of available coal rather larger; but enough has been said to show that the sub-marine areas form an important addition to the visible coal field.* The seams appear on the shore, sweep inland, and again enter the ocean, forming segments of irregular ellipses, whose centres are miles out at sea. This peculiar formation is repeated at Cow Bay, Glace Bay, Lingan, Sydney, and Campbelltown, and presents a number of almost independent basins, the correlation of whose seams was long a puzzle to those engaged in developing the districts.

After a careful survey, extending over a number of years, Mr. H. Fletcher, of the Geo. Sur., has demonstrated the equivalence of several of the seams of this district formerly regarded as distinct. The following table shows, in a condensed form, the views he arrived at, which, although differing from the arrangements proposed by other Geologists, may be regarded as correct.

---

* For further information, see "Sub-marine Coal of Cape Breton," by E. Gilpin. Trans.: North of England Institute, 1875.

Tabular View of Seams of Sydney Coal Field.

COW BAY.	GLACE BAY.	LINGAN.		SYDNEY MINES.	BOULARDERIE.
SEAM.	SEAM.	SEAM.	Strata & Coal ft. in.	SEAM.	SEAM.
....	....	Seam A.......	3.0 306.0	....	Point Aconi.
....	....	Carr..........	6.5 190.0	Lloyd's Cove..	Bonar.
....	Hub	Barrasois	12.1 379.3	Seam B.......	Stubbart.
Block House........	Harbour.........	{ Victoria, David Hd. }	8.0 235.0 3.0	{ Sydney Main	Seam C.
Seam D...........	Bouthilier........	Seam D.......	78.0 4.0	Bryant........	Mill Pond.
Seam E...........	Back Pit.........	North Head..	75.0 8.0	Edward........	Black Rock.
McAulay..........	Phelan..........	Lingan Main..	95.0	Seam F.......	Seam F.
South Head, Spencer, }	{ Ross, ... Emery........ }	Seam G.......	4.6 340.0	{ Collins'	Seam G.
Long Beach........	{ Lorway, ... Gardener .... }	Seam H.......	4.9	....	

The exceptional freedom from faults which characterises this coal field has been strongly dwelt upon by all who have been engaged in exploring it. Prof. Lesley, in reporting on the Little Glace Bay district, says: "The water level lines of the beds are now seen to be parallel, and the whole country wonderfully level, and free from faults." This remark applies equally to the other districts, and adds materially to the confidence with which mining operations are begun.

I have not given the thickness of the seams and associated strata in each district, as the dimensions of the Lingan section answer fairly for the rest. There are other seams found underlying these, and varying in thickness from two to eight feet; but I will not notice them further than to say that the fossils associated with some of the beds would indicate an extension of the productive or true coal measures much further to the westward than was generally believed to be the case.

Taking the seams as given in the table in descending order, we have first to notice seam A, which has not yet been worked. Although the land area of this seam is small, it is believed that it will be found accessible under the sea for a long distance.

The Lloyd's Cove seam was opened by the General Mining Association in their Sydney area, some years ago, and workings were extended over about 18 acres, but it being found that the Main seam could meet all demands, it was abandoned.

The Hub seam was opened and extensively worked by the Little Glace Bay Co. some years ago. The land area of this seam is about 150 acres, 60 of which have been partly worked out, leaving a large amount of good coal; but all operations are now abandoned. The accessible sea area of this seam is estimated at 2,500 acres, yielding 35 millions of tons of coal.

The coal from this seam is well adapted for gas making, the quantity per ton varying from 9,500 to 10,000 cubic feet of 15 candle power. The residual coke is of excellent quality.

From an official report on the coal from this seam and the underlying or Harbor bed worked by the same Company, made to the Admiralty, it appears that the former contains 80·9, and the latter 83·5 per cent. of Carbon, and are theoretically equal to Welsh coal, which is borne out by practical tests. Both of the coals were found to light quickly, make steam fast, and to give a moderate amount of clinker and ash, the only drawback that was mentioned being the fact that they yielded a considerable amount of smoke. From trials that have been made since, in England and the United States, it has been shewn that, with proper draft and furnace arrangements, the bituminous coals of the class under consideration can readily be burnt, not only without producing smoke, but with a correspondingly increased evaporative power.

The slack coal from the Hub seam was made into coke to a small extent some years ago. The quality was said to be excellent, and to have but little Sulphur; but I am not aware of any analysis having been made.

The next seam on the list has been extensively worked by the Block House, Little Glace Bay, International, Victoria, and Sydney Collieries.

The coal from the Block House Mine has yielded at the New York and Boston gas-works 10,316 cubic feet of 16½ candle gas, and 1,460 ℔s. of coke; and large quantities of it have been sold for that purpose in these markets.

It has also proved a capital steam coal, and when tried on board H. M. S. Gannet, was found to raise steam fifteen minutes quicker than any other coal that had been supplied to the ship. When mixed with twice its weight of Tillery Elled Welsh Coal, a saving of 12 per cent. over the Welsh coal alone, was reported. The per-centage of ash and clinker was very small.

At the works of the Little Glace Bay Co. this seam has recently been opened at a lower level, and the quality of the coal found to improve. The following are the Gas values of the coal, as determined during the past year:

Montreal New City Gas Co.	*Halifax Gas Co.*
Gas, cubic ft., per ton......9,268	Gas, cubic ft., per ton......9,700
Candle Power............ 15	Candle Power............14·75
Coke (good) bus........... 40	Coke (very good) bus....... 39

I have already spoken of the fitness of this coal for use in the English Navy, and remark here that the results would be found higher from the coal at present mined.

At the International Mine, on the South side of Lingan Bay, this seam differs little from its characteristics observable in the Glace Bay Stirling Pit. The quality of the coal is very good, being compact and free from shale. It has been used chiefly for gas in New York; and has been successfully introduced for the same purpose into the Montreal and Ottawa markets. It has yielded 10,000 cubic feet of gas of 16 candle power, and 1,470 ℔s. of good coke to the ton. It has also been satisfactorily used for a steam coal, and certified equal to best West Hartley, the only drawback being a clinker apt to adhere to the furnace bars.

From trials made during 1879, and noticed in speaking of the Pictou coals, it appears that this coal is well adapted for locomotive work, and is highly recommended by those in charge of the tests.

At the Victoria Mine the seam is more compact, and loses to some extent the bright, pitchy appearance it presents to the South. The coal is not recommended for gas making, but is found to be a capital steam and house fuel, and has never been known to heat in cargo. It has not been tried for coke; but the slack finds sale for steam and blacksmiths' work.

At the Sydney Mines of the General Mining Association, this seam has proved of excellent quality for steam and domestic use. The estimation it is held in for the latter purpose may be judged of by the fact that it retails in Halifax at a price 30 to 80 cts. higher per chaldron than any other Cape Breton coal.

The following are the average results of four trials of its gas values at Halifax:

Gas, cubic ft., per ton................	8,200
Candle Power.......................	8
Coke (good) ℔s.....................	1,295

It has been pronounced by the Engineers of the French Navy equal to the best Newcastle, for steam-raising, and has been extensively used by mail and other vessels for a number of years.

The following is the result of a trial of this coal made by the American Government in 1841, and is, as far as I am aware, the only practical trial that has been made of the evapórative power of any of the Cape Breton coals :

Moisture .... 3·13	Lbs. of water to one of coal,	
Volatile Comb: Matter......23·81	from 212°................7·90	
Fixed Carbon............. 67·57	Ash and Clinker, per cent... 6·00	
Ash .... 5·49	Theoretical Evap. Power.... 9·25*	

The following analyses show the composition of this seam, as worked at the Collieries noticed above :

COMPOSITION.†	BLOCK HOUSE.	HARBOR.	VICTORIA.	SYDNEY.
Moisture........................	·600	·80	·28	1·260
Vol: Comb: Matter, Fast Coking.....	31·580	29·40	33·30	35·514
Fixed Carbon " "	63·465	65·50	62·92	59·111
Vol: Comb: Matter, Slow "	29·480	27·85	28·61	33·840
Fixed Carbon, " "	65·565	67·05	67.61	60·785
Ash.............................	4·355	4·30	3·50	4·115
Sulphur.........................	2·630	2·32	2·84	1·705
Specific Gravity..................	1·292	1·29	1·29	1·312
Theo: Evap: Power, Fast Coking.....	8·99	8·98	8·63	8·14
" " " Slow "	8·97	9·19	9·27	8·33

The two following seams, known as the Bouthilier and Back Pit of Glace Bay, and the Mill Pond and Black Rock of Boularderie, vary in thickness from 3 to 6 feet, and have been traced from end to end of the coal field. Although of good quality, they have hitherto been neglected in the presence of the larger seams, and may at this date be considered an important reserve. I regret that I am not in possession of any analyses or other positive information relating to these seams in the Southern part of the district, beyond the records of sinking pits and exploratory slopes, which agree in describing them as being suitable for steam and domestic use. The only opening in them is that made by Mr. Campbell, at Cape Dauphin, where the equivalent of the Black Rock seam has been worked. At this point the seam is 4 ft. 6 in. thick, and finds a market in Halifax and other Provincial ports as being adapted for house use.

All the evaporative powers, as given in this report, are calculated from Regnault's formula.

† Unless otherwise specified, the coal and ash analyses are by the writer, and taken from a paper on "Canadian Coals, their Composition and Uses," communicated by him to the North of England Mining Institute, 1878.

The next seam on the list is known as the McAulay, Phelan, and Lingan, and is worked by the Gowrie, Ontario, Caledonia, Reserve, and Lingan Collieries.

This valuable bed has furnished a large amount of coal, and may be considered the typical seam of the district.

At the Gowrie Colliery the seam is 5 ft. 2 in. thick. The product is used for steam and domestic purposes, and has been found adapted for iron working. From certificates given by engineers and masters of steamers, the coal is considered superior to all English coals, except the Welsh, for evaporative power. Its freedom from clinker, and low percentage of ash, and the consequent absence of injury to fire bars, are specially dwelt upon.

In the retorts of the New York Gas Co., it yielded 9,000 cubic ft. of gas of 15 candle power, and 1,230 lbs. of good coke to the ton, and 2,100 cubic ft. were purified by one bushel of lime.

At the Ontario and Caledonia Mines, this seam varies its character slightly, and becomes, although still a good gas coal, rather more free burning, and holds slightly above the ordinary per-centage of ash found in the Cape Breton coals.

The Caledonia coal has been largely exported to the New England States for steam and gas purposes, and also for lime burning and domestic use. In 1878 it yielded, at the Montreal Gas-works, per ton of 2,000 lbs., 8,900 cubic ft. of 14·25 candle power, and 36 bushels of fair coke.

At the Reserve Mine it forms one of the handsomest of the Cape Breton coals, and is used chiefly for steam purposes. A considerable amount is sent to Newfoundland, where it is in demand for sealing steamers, which require a coal capable of raising steam rapidly.

It has yielded, as a gas coal, 9,950 cubic ft. of 13·17 candle gas, and 1,500 lbs. of coke per ton. 2,380 cubic ft. are purified by one bushel of lime.

At Lingan this seam laid the foundation of the gas reputation of the Cape Breton coals in the United States. Large quantities were exported to New York and Boston for this purpose, but it shares the late depression. It is said to yield from 9,000 to 10,000 cubic ft. of $15\frac{1}{2}$ candle power gas per ton. It has also been used to a considerable extent for house use, and should prove an excellent steam coal.

The coal was carefully tried on the steam dredge "St. Lawrence, employed last summer in deepening the approaches to the wharf; and the engineer, after referring in flattering terms to its steady and good steaming qualities, and small amount of ash, winds up by saying that he preferred it to any coal he had used.

The following table shows the composition of this seam at the various collieries now working:

COMPOSITION.	GOWRIE.	CALEDONIA.	RESERVE.	LINGAN.
Moisture	·50	·921	·52	·75
Vol: Com: Matter, Fast Coking	31·41	30·312	37·60	37·26
Fixed Carbon, " "	62·73	62·334	56·34	58·74
Vol: Com: Matter, Slow "	28·13	28·625	34·21	34·61
Fixed Carbon, " "	66·01	64·021	59·73	61·39
Ash	5·36	6·433	5·54	3·25
Sulphur	2·71	1·105	1·25	1·35
Specific Gravity	1·31	1·330	1·28	1·29
Theo. Evap. Power, Fast Coking	8·62	8·62	7·86	8·00
" " " Slow "	9·05	8·78	8·19	8·42

The next seam on the list has been opened at all points in the district; but owing to several causes, operations are at present suspended. The coal from the South Head Colliery should, from its appearance, prove a good steam coal, and has yielded 8,000 cubic ft. of 16 candle gas from a sample cargo. The coal from the openings at the Schooner Pond, Emery, and Collins' Collieries is also reported to be adapted for gas purposes, but I am not in possession of any detailed experiments.

The lowest seam that has been developed is known as the Lorway or Gardener, and has been worked at these two mines. It has been found a good steam coal, well adapted for ships' use, as it is not smoky, nor does it form a clinker in any way injuring the fire bars.

The following table shows the composition of these seams:

COMPOSITION.	SOUTH HEAD	EMERY.	COLLINS.	GARDENER.
Moisture	1·767	·65	1·983	....
Vol: Comb: Matter, Fast Coking	28·833	34·80	30·896	....
Fixed Carbon, " "	61·430	60·90	61·742	....
Vol: Comb: Matter, Slow Coking	28·000	32·21	26·156	31·96
Fixed Carbon, " "	62·263	63·49	66·482	65·22
Ash	7·970	3·65	5·397	2·82
Sulphur	2·641	2·41	2·248	1·18
Specific Gravity	1·382	1·287	1·311	....
Theo: Evap: Power, Fast Coking	8·42	8·25	8·43	....
" " " Slow "	8·53	8·70	9·10	....

But little can be said at present of the seams underlying the Gardener, as they are known only by pits and natural exposures. They include several beds of good quality, as shown by the following analyses from

[1] Geo. Sur. Rep. 1872-3.

the G. S. R. 1874-5, and as a demand arises will doubtless receive more attention.

The Tracey seam was worked some years ago, and is said to be equal in quality to any previously noticed.

The Fraser seam is a Canneloid coal, giving an intense heat; and the Carroll seam is described as suited for coke and blacksmiths' use.

	TRACEY SEAM. 4 ft. 2 in.	FRASER SEAM. 6 ft. 4 in.	CARROLL SEAM. 7 ft. 2 in.
Moisture	2·23	....	....
Vol: Comb: Matter	30·09	31·4	32·8
Fixed Carbon	66·61	62·4	61·4
Ash	·98	6·2	5·8
	99·91	100·0	100·0

The following ultimate analyses have been made of coals from this district:

COMPOSITION.	BLOCK HOUSE.'	RESERVE.†	SCHOONER POND.†
Carbon	82·60	77·41	78·10
Hydrogen	4·79	5·47	5·48
Nitrogen	1·20	} 9·30	} 7·81
Oxygen	4·10		
Sulphur	2·51	2·47	2·49
Ash	4·80	4·35	3·45
Water	....	1·00	2·67
	100·00	100·00	100·00

The nature of the ash of the Cape Breton coals may be gathered from the following analyses, by the writer:

COMPOSITION.	BLOCK HOUSE.	CALEDONIA.	VICTORIA.	EMERY.
Iron peroxide	45·621	11·853	56·543	38·764
Alumina	3·250	4·200	6·456	1·336
Insoluble Silicious residue	35·110	65·734	27·500	50·673
Manganese	....	·950	1·930	trace.
Magnesia	1·100	1·260	·035	1·015
Lime	5·425	7·151	2·598	4·200
Sulphuric Acid	6·750	4·283	3·790	4·030
Phosphoric Acid	1·900	2·725	·691	·012
Alkalies	trace.	2·150	·150	trace.
Chlorine	....	trace.	....	....
	99·156	100·306	99·693	100·030

' Made for the Admiralty, at Halifax.
† Royal School of Mines.

From the preceeding remarks and analyses, it will be seen that this district furnishes coal particularly suited for gas making. It is, also, as appears from the notices of certificates, equal to the coal furnished to the English Mercantile Navy, being considered as almost equal to Welsh steam coal, which may be ranked as the standard for comparison.

The enormous amount of available coal it contains may be estimated from the Geological Survey Report, which states that the seams now opened contain, in the areas leased for the purpose of working them, over 212,000,000 tons.

This estimate does not include the coal in the seams which are unopened in the land areas, in operation, nor the values of the seams on the leases which are at present awaiting a favorable opportunity for development, which items would swell the total quantity of coal in the Sydney district to a volume which assures very many years supply at rates far exceeding the present annual out-put.

The coal available, will long form an important and increasing source of revenue to the Government, and give to manufacturing industries the assurance of an abundant supply, at uniform prices, which is always an important consideration.

These coals are also well adapted for house use, and are extensively used in Halifax and the neighboring colonies for that purpose; moreover, they furnish coke, which has been made to a small extent at Little Glace Bay and Sydney, and proved of good quality. In the event of any demand arising for this article, large quantities could be furnished at a low price.

There are a number of seams of cannel coal scattered through the coal measures, varying in thickness up to 2 feet. They are in some instances considered valuable, but as yet no openings have been made on them.

The measures enclosing the Cape Breton coals are largely composed of argillaceous shales and sandstones, frequently occurring in thick beds, the latter sometimes intercalated with girdles and bands of ironstone. A few beds of limestone and conglomerates are met, but they do not form an important per-centage. This solidity and coherence of the strata, always an essential item in mining, becomes specially valuable in view of the present and future extent of sub-marine operations in the district I have been considering.

The systems of mining adopted in this coal field vary, from the extensive and well planned establishment of the General Mining

Association at North Sydney, with its large underground and winding engines, massive pumps and ventilating fans, all contributing to effect an output of 900 or 1000 tons a day, down to a small colliery raising some 150 tons a day with a little portable engine, and dependent on the caprices of the atmosphere for its ventilation.

Artificial harbours and breakwaters have been made at Glace and Cow Bays, by several of the companies, while others ship at Sydney Harbour. The Cape Breton Coal Company have commenced shipments at Louisburg, and it is to be hoped that this fine harbour will soon be extensively used as an all winter shipping place, not only for the proprietors of the Cape Breton Company's Mines, but also for other companies.

The cost of the coal, mined and put into cars, varies at the different collieries from 60 cents to $1.25; the transport and shipping, and interest on capital being different in each case. Surface labourers receive from 85 cts. to $1.00, mechanics $1.10 to $1.50 a day. The wages of the coal cutters, who are paid by contract, vary from $1.25 to $1.75 per working day. Provisions, lumber, land, etc., are easily and cheaply procured, and few countries offer better facilities for opening coal mines.

INVERNESS.

Inverness Coal Field.—From Cheticamp to Judique, on the Western shore of Cape Breton, there extends a narrow and broken line of productive measures, forming the edges of great basins of coal, which have long ago disappeared beneath the Gulf of St. Lawrence.

At Chimney Corner, Prof. Hynd reported two groups of seams, nothing being known of the lower. The upper gave the following section:

	ft.	in.
Thin Seams	1	6
Strata	300	0
Coal	3	0
Strata	88	0
Coal	5	0
Strata	200	0
Coal	3	6

The measures here form a sharp synclinal, about three quarters of a mile wide, giving an estimated land area of about 5 square miles; however, but little is yet known of the extent of the seams of the lower group.

At Broad Cove, about 10 miles to the south-west, the following section of seams, contained in about 2000 feet of strata, is said to exist, and is given on Mr. A. Wright's authority.

First	Seam	2 feet	
Second	"	2 "	
Third	"	3 "	McKinnon Brook.
Fourth	"	4 "	"
Fifth	"	12 "	
Sixth	"	7 "	Seam now worked.
Seventh	"	4 "	Big River.
Eighth	"	3 "	"

Operations have been confined to the 7 foot seam, from which a few tons have been shipped to Moncton and Prince Edward Island.

The extent of productive measures here is not yet positively known, but areas embracing about twenty square miles, believed to hold workable coal, have been secured by various parties.

In the Geo. Sur. Rep. 1874, p. 183, it is stated: "Judging from appearance, the coal, which is of the bituminous kind, seems to be of excellent quality. From the manner in which it burns in a common fire, I should judge it to be peculiarly free from liability to produce dense black smoke." The coal has been satisfactorily burnt for house and steam purposes. The district at present labors under the disadvantage of having no proper shipping ground. It is proposed to remedy this by opening McIsaac's Pond, about one mile distant, which operation, if successful, would provide good loading facilities, and a harbor of refuge for this section of the Island.

Another of these small, but valuable, coal fields occurs at Mabou; here the outcrops of the following beds are reported, namely, a 4 foot bed, a 13 foot bed, about 20 feet above the first, a 7 foot seam 120 (?) feet higher, and a 5 foot seam. There are also several other seams, the size and extent of which are unknown. The usual basin shape is presented here with an area somewhat smaller than at Broad Cove.

At Port Hood one seam only has been definitely tested, although the presence of several others has been proved. Here the strata run more nearly parallel with the shore, and extend along it about 2 miles. The seam opened has a thickness of 6 feet. Workings were pushed a short distance under the sea, but are discontinued at present. The outcrop of another 6 feet seam is known at low water. Coal occurs again at Little Judique, in close proximity to gypsum and limestone.

The following analyses will show the character of these coals:

COMPOSITION.	CHIMNEY CORNER.*	BROAD COVE.		PORT HOOD.‡
		7 foot seam.†	5 foot seam.†	
Water...........................	8·19	4·02	7·24	25·35
Vol: Com: Matter, Fast Coking......	26·39	25·39	32·43	316·52
Fixed Carbon, "	57·70	65·19	50·18	600·86
Vol: Comb: Matter, Slow Coking.....	....	20·17	25·75	298·15
Fixed Carbon, " ......:...	....	70·41	56·86	619·23
Ash.............................	7·72	5·40	10·15	57·27
Sulphur.........................	....	....	1·41	55·4
Theo: Evap: Power, Fast Coking.....	7·89	....	6·81	82·3
" " " Slow "	....	....	7·61	84·9

From these analyses it will be seen that the seams, although holding more than the normal per-centages of water, are of good quality, and would command a fair share of the Canadian markets, if a proper outlet were provided. At present there is no harbor where they can be shipped, and it is to be hoped that attempts will be made to provide suitable facilities, as the opening of mines along this shore would prove a great benefit to the district generally, which is almost entirely cut off from a market.

Mr. Richard Brown, in his "Coal Fields of Cape Breton," very properly remarks : " Immediate steps should be taken by the Government to ascertain the exact position of the coal seams of Inverness ; because, owing to the rapid wearing away of the shore, all traces of these seams will soon become obliterated." In proof of this, Seal Island may be cited, which, composed of Carboniferous strata, and once, beyond all doubt, connected with the mainland, is now separated by a channel two miles broad.

It is evident, therefore, that a belt of coast, at least two miles wide, has disappeared, effacing the outcrops of many valuable seams. Port Hood is another instance of the wasting powers of the Gulf of St. Lawrence.

If correct plans are now made, showing the position of every seam, at a future date, when their outcrops have disappeared, they may be won by sub-marine tunnels, started from the shore.

RICHMOND.

Little River Coal Field.—In Richmond County a number of years ago, extensive explorations were carried on, and a few hundred tons of coal extracted from seams, which have since been neglected.

* Dr. H. How.   † Geo. Sur. Rep. 1874.   ‡ E. Gilpin.

This district is considered to extend from a point 8 miles above the new bridge on the River Inhabitants to Little River and Sea Coal Bay, on the west, and Coal Brook on the east side of River Inhabitants basin. This district has recently been carefully surveyed by Mr. H. Fletcher, of the Geological Survey, and doubtless his report and map will accurately define the value and extent of the coal-bearing strata.

The seams opened on the Sea Coal Cove include one 11 feet thick, inclusive of several bands of shale, and two, 4 and 5 feet in thickness, the latter having a band of fire clay in the centre.

At Richmond, on the Little River, 2½ miles north-east of Sea Coal Cove, two seams, four feet thick, and 150 feet apart, have been opened. About seven miles above the River Inhabitants' new bridge a bed of coal 1 ft. 8 in. thick, underlaid by 2 ft. 3 in. of coaly shale, is exposed. The crops of other seams are reported on the River Inhabitants, Coal Brook, etc.; but there is not much known about them.

The position of the gypsum and limestones of this district, relative to the coal beds, raises a doubt whether the coal of this county should be considered as belonging to the productive or to the lower measures of the carboniferous series.

The following analyses of these coals were made a number of years ago by Dr. Dawson:

	11 foot Seam, Seal Coal Cove.	4 foot Bed.
Volatile Matter	25·2	30·25
Fixed Carbon	44·7	56·40
Ash	30·1	13·35
	100·0	100·00

ANTIGONISH.

A few miles north of Antigonish a small coal field was found some years ago. Enough work was done to show the presence of five seams, varying in thickness from 3 to 6 feet, accompanied by beds of oil shale. The coal is said to be of fair quality; but I have not heard of any analyses or practical tests which would serve to show what position it may be expected to assume among the other coals. At present, there is not demand enough to render its extraction advisable, in the presence of the Halifax and Cape Breton Railway which, starting from New Glasgow, carries the Pictou coal through the centre of Antigonish County. In the event of industries being started requiring any large quantity of coal, such as copper smelting, etc., it may be expected to add another to our list of productive districts. Its area is variously estimated at from 5 to 10 square miles; but as so little work has been done, no positive information can be given on this point.

THE PICTOU COAL FIELD.

This district lies immediately south of the town of New Glasgow, in Pictou County. The area of the field may be estimated at about 35 square miles, and it extends from a point near Sutherland's River to the Middle River of Pictou. This area, although comparatively limited, contains a large amount of coal, owing to the unusual size of the beds, and the good exposures of their crops. The district may be roughly described as forming a main east and west synclinal, disturbed and shifted by minor north and south undulations, which expose the outcrops of the seams in irregular curves and basins.

The forces producing our gold field anticlinals would seem to have extended into this district, as well as into the Cumberland coal field, and produce irregularities which, before they were understood, caused much confusion in the tracing and correllation of the seams.

The former extent of this coal field must have been very considerably larger. It now forms an irregular basin, let down on all sides among rocks of older age. When we consider that, in the Albion Mines' district, there is a section of measures 2,450 feet in vertical thickness, holding 100 feet of coal, lying at an angle of 18°, denuded to a horizontal plane, it is evident that this great mass of sediments, when lying undisturbed, must have stretched a considerable distance over what are now the boundary rocks.

From the information at present available, the seams of this district may be divided into an upper and lower group, all included in 5,567 feet of measures, according to Sir W. Logan.* The upper group contains the following beds:

	Strata. ft. in.	Coal. ft. in.
Captain Seam............	....	4·0
Intermediate......................	108·0	....
Millrace................	....	4·0
do.	53·0	....
Geo. McKay.............	....	4·10

* For further information, see Geo. Sur. Rep. 1869; Papers by the writer, in the transactions of the Nova Scotia Institute of Natural Science, in the grouping of the Pictou Coal Seams, etc. Also, a paper on the Pictou Coal Field; North of England Institute of Mining Engineers, 1873; Coal Fields of Nova Scotia; J. Rutherford, ibid; Acadian Geology, etc.

		Strata. ft. in.	Coal. ft. in.
Intermediate		600·0 (?)	....
	Seam	....	6.0
do.		800.0	....
	McBean	....	8·0
do.		80.0	....
	Pottery	....	2·9
do.		760·0	....
	Stewart... } McLennan }	....	4·0

The three first-mentioned seams occur as a small basin, in the eastern part of the district, and they are also believed to occur again as a small basin immediately in the rear of New Glasgow, while it is not yet settled whether the six and eight foot seams crop in the interval between the two basins or re-appear only near New Glasgow. This uncertainty is owing to the fact that little exploratory work has been done in this part of the coal field.

These upper seams are best proved on the property of the Vale Coal Co.; and by the kindness of J. B. Moore, Esq., Vice-President of that Company, I am enabled to present the following analyses of them, made by me for him two years ago, from samples procured on that area:

Composition.	North Crop, G. McKay.	South Crop, G. McKay.	Greener, or 6 ft. Seam.	McBean.	Pottery or Moore.
Moisture	1·62	·90	1·22	·86	·57
Vol: Comb: Mat:, Fast Coking	29·89	30·36	25·87	25·87	26.65
Fixed Carbon, " "	61.15	57·42	62·70	60·03	65·35
Vol: Comb: Mat:, Slow "	22·86	22·50	22·96	20·95	19·24
Fixed Carbon, " "	68·18	65·28	65·61	64·95	72·76
Ash	7·34	11·32	10·21	13·24	7·43
Sulphur	·53	1·72	trace.	·85	·65
Theo:Evap: Pow:, Fast Coking	8·39	7·87	8·59	8.23	8·98
" " " Slow "	9·35	8·97	8·99	8·90	9·97

From the above analyses, it will be seen that all these coals are of excellent quality, the Geo. McKay and Moore seams being apparently suitable for gas and coke making; while all of them have small percentages of Sulphur, and a very high evaporative power. The McBean seam has been extensively worked at the Vale Colliery, and has proved well adapted for steam raising in marine and stationary, as well as locomotive, engines.

The President of the Moisie Iron Works writes, that it is admirably adapted for iron making, as the grates require cleaning only once a day.

The Manager of the Richelieu and Ontario Navigation Co. states that, "the coal makes no clinker, and is easy on the grates; and lasts longer than Scotch. I consider it equal to Scotch coal in its results."

The Q. M. O. & O. R. R. authorities find that, when mixed with Scotch coal, the results are higher than if the coals are burned separately.

Nearer home the coal has been largely used on the Intercolonial Railway, and the steamers of the Allan Line.

The upper group is represented on the western side of the East River by the small seams lying along the axis of the Albion synclinal, and not at present considered as occupying an area requiring extended notice.

The lower group, hidden in the Eastern district by the measures holding the seams just described, has been extensively worked to the west of the East River, and presents the following section:

		Ft. In.	Ft. In.
	Main Seam	34.7	....
Strata	....	....	148.0
	Deep Seam	22.11	....
do.	....	....	106.8
	Third Seam	5.7	....
do.	....	....	113.0
	Purvis Seam	3.6	....
do.	....	....	130.0
	Fleming Seam	3.3	....
do.	....	....	4.3
	McGregor Seam	12.0	....
do.	....	....	211.9
	Stellar Seam	5.0	....
do.	....	....	15.0
	Seam A	11.0	....
do.	....	....	187.6
	Seam C	10.0	....

There are other underlying seams which, with seams A and C, have not yet been tested, and are known only as outcrops.

The Main Seam has been worked for many years at the Albion Mines by the Halifax Coal Company and their predecessors. The Acadia Seam of Westville, operated by the Acadia, Intercolonial, and Nova Scotia Coal Cos., is considered to be, if not an extension, at any rate the equivalent, of the Main Seam. The general form of the Main Seam is that of an irregular synclinal, the north edge of which has been proved on the Montreal and Pictou area, opposite New Glasgow;

while as yet all mining operations have been confined to the southern outcrop.

The seam opened at Culton's Mill Pond, to the south-east of the Intercolonial Colliery, is believed to represent the extreme southerly extension of the Main and other seams in that part of the district.

The coal from this seam at the Albion Mines is well known as a very good steam coal; and also yields a coke of good quality, which has been successfully used at the Londonderry blast furnaces. The following analysis is given, compared with Connelsville coke, which is considered the American standard for this class of fuel:

	Albion Mines.[*]	Connelsville.[†]
Moisture	·96	·52
Carbon	83·85	85·24
Sulphur	·52	·69
Phosphoric Acid	·01	·029
Ash	14·50	12.30

The coke is hard, resistant, and well provided with cell spaces.

Large quantities of this coal were, some years ago, exported to the United States for gas making, and the following analyses of two samples from the north and south side of the Foord pit dip workings show that it still maintains its character in this respect:

Analyses made at the London Gas Light and Coke Co's. Works, 1879, gave

10,300 and 10,450 cubic ft. of 15 candle power gas, and
14 cwt. 2 qrs. of good coke per ton of 2,240 lbs.

At the Works of the Pictou Gas Co., this coal yielded gas generally exceeding by one or two per cent. the legal illuminating power, which is fixed at sixteen candles, and proved very free from sulphur when the purifiers were attended to.

Two samples of coal from Pictou were tested at the American Navy trials in 1843. The coals must have been from the Albion Mines, working the Main and Deep seams, there being no others then opened; but it is not stated which seam they represented.

The following are the results, from Mr. Walter Johnstone's "Coal Trade of British America," page 134:

	Ash in Furnace.	Lbs. of Steam from 212° F.	Theo: Evap: Pow:[‡]
No. 1	13·37	8·41	7·63
No. 2	12·06	8·48	8·33

[*] Average three Analyses.   [†] J. B. Britton, New York.
[‡] Regnault's formula.

At the Intercolonial Colliery the coal is of a similar character—yielding a merchantable coke, of which I regret I have no analysis; and proving well adapted for steam raising, for which purpose it has been extensively used on the Intercolonial Railway, and various steamers. It is also a good mill coal, and large quantities have been sent to Montreal for this purpose. From careful tests, it has been proved to evaporate 7·69 lbs. of water from 212° F. for every pound of coal burnt.*

From trials made on the Gulf Port steamer "Secret," and others, the coal has received a very high character. The latest gas analysis that I have seen gives its yield at 7,000 cubic ft. of 15 candle power, with 34 bush. of good coke. It has also been extensively used as a house coal. At the Acadia Colliery the coal is of a rather more free burning character; but it is on a par with the others as a good steam coal, under all conditions of use. From careful practical trials on a locomotive, it has been found capable of evaporating 7·24 lbs. of water from 212° F. for every pound of coal burnt.

It has been extensively used for steam purposes in Nova Scotia and elsewhere. It is also in good demand as a domestic fuel, and its sale for this purpose is increased by the care taken in its preparation.

At the Nova Scotia Colliery, not at present working, the coal is very similar in adaptability, and has been extensively exported for the same uses to the United States and Montreal.

The following table shows the composition of this fine seam at the various Collieries which have been opened on it:

Composition.	Albion Mines.	Acadia.†	Inter-colonial.	Nova Scotia.‡
Moisture	1·05	2·10	1·52	....
Vol: Com: Matter, Fast Coking	27·42	32·78	31·87	....
Fixed Carbon, " "	62·18	57·57	57·78	....
Vol: Com: Matter, Slow " "	26·19	29·20	29·46	32·68
Fixed Carbon, " " "	63·41	61·15	60·19	62·08
Ash	9·35	7·55	9·10	5·24
Sulphur	1·48	·506	1·625	trace.
Specific Gravity	1·31	1·32	1·33	....
Theo: Evap: Power, Fast Coking	8·49	....	7·92	....
" " " Slow "	8·68	....	8·24	8·57

The Deep or Cage Pit Seam has been worked only at the Albion Mines, whence large quantities have been exported for steam purposes

* Geo: Sur: Rep:, 1869, p. 398.
† Geo: Sur: Rep:, 1869, p. 381.   ‡ Prof. Silliman, Yale College.

and iron working, many customers preferring to have it mixed with the Main Seam coal, as the steam-raising power of the mixture is believed to exceed that of either coal burnt individually.

The McGregor Seam was formerly worked by the Acadia Colliery; the coal was considered specially adapted for steam purposes, and its theoretical evaporative power was as high as 9·62 lbs.

The Stellar oil Coal, formerly worked by the same Company, is a very high class Cannel Coal.

The Stellarite, varying in thickness from 6 to 24 inches, has above it 1 ft. 4 in. of fat bituminous coal, and is underlaid by about the same thickness of oil shale.

The following analyses of the Stellarite and Oil Shale are by Prof. Wallace, of Glasgow:

	Stellarite.	Oil Shale.
Volatile Matter	68·38	38·69
Fixed Carbon	22·35	8·26
Ash	8·90	52·20
Sulphur	·05	·25
Moisture	·32	·60
Specific Gravity	1·079	1·568
Crude Oil, per ton, gals.	126	63
Gravity of Oil	·844	·850
Coke, per cent	31·25	60·46

For comparison, the following results are submitted, from Dr. How's Mineralogy of Nova Scotia:

	Crude Oil per ton.
Union Oil Coal of West Virginia affords	32 gallons.
Elk River " " " "	54 "
Kanawha " " " "	88 "
Lesmahagow Cannel, Scotland, "	40 "
Albertite, New Brunswick, "	92 to 100 "
Torbanite, Scotland, "	116 to 125 "
Stellarite, or "Stellar Coal" "	53 "
" " No. 2..50, 60¾, 63, 65, 74 "
" " No. 1	123 to 126 "
" " Picked samples gave in Boston	199 "

An ultimate analyses of the Stellarite gave Prof. Anderson, of Glasgow: Carbon, 80·96; Hydrogen, 10·15; Nitrogen, Sulphur, and Oxygen, ·68; Ash, 8·21.

In practical working at the mine, 60 gals. of crude and 35 of refined oil were obtained. This material is also well adapted for a gas enricher, being similar to Torbanite, and the New Brunswick Albertite.

In addition to the Stellar Seam, there are several beds of oil shale known in this coal field, on the property of the Pictou Companies; but in the presence of native Canadian and American oils, they cannot at present be worked with profit.

The following analyses of the Deep and other seams will be of interest:

Composition.	Deep.	McGregor* 2nd Bench.	Ms'h. Brk.* Oil Shale.	Montreal & Pictou.†
Moisture	·75	} 23·30	5·96	5·47
Vol: Comb: Matter, Fast Coking	25·82		40·00	19·93
Fixed Carbon, " "	63·02	70·00	·40	68·55
Vol: Comb: Matter, Slow Coking	20·34	....	35·00	....
Fixed Carbon, " "	68·50	....	5·26	....
Ash	10·41	6·70	59·20	6·05
Sulphur	·945	....	....	....
Specific Gravity	1·33	1·301	1·68	1·36
Theo: Evap: Power, Fast Coking	8·64	9·62	....	9·41
" " " Slow "	9·39	....	....	....

The following analyses of the ash from Pictou Coals will be found interesting for comparison with those from Cape Breton:

Composition.	Main Seam.	Deep Seam.	McBean Seam.
Iron peroxide	·500	7·115	} 7·890
Alumina	5·350	10·000	
Sand and Clay (Insol:)	36·821	72·000	{ 54·300 33·200
Lime	1·200	4·212	·985
Magnesia	trace.	2·650	·155
Manganese	·155	none.	none.
Sulphuric Acid	·500	2·225	·785
Phosphoric Acid	1·222	1·895	1·500
Chlorine	none.	none.	none.
Alkalies	trace.	traces.	traces.
	100·000	100·000	98·875

From the foregoing analyses and remarks, it will be seen that some of the Pictou Coals are adapted for gas making, and have been successfully used for that purpose; although, as a class they may not be called gas coals. They are all well adapted for steam purposes, and have been extensively used on Nova Scotian and Canadian Railways.

The following table shows the results arrived at by careful trials

* Northern outcrop of Main Seam, worked at the Albion Mines.
† Geo: Sur; Rep:, 1869.

made on the Q. M. O. & O. R. R., during the year 1879, by Mr. A. Davis, Mechanical Superintendent:

Coal Tested.	Date.	Miles run to 1 ton of coal.	Coal in lbs. per car, per mile.	Lbs. of Ash, per cent.	Miles run.	Depth of Fire. Inches.
Pictou Co. Albion Mine.	June 6, 7, 6, 10,	78	4·11	13·0	480	10-16
Intercolonial	16, 17, 18, 19	82	4·70	12·5	"	8-10
Vale	July 2, 3, 4, 5.	80	4·90	12·5	"	10-16
Acadia	4, 5, 8, 9.	80	4·90	13·0	"	10-16
Cape Breton. International	June 6, 7, 9, 10	81	4·80	14·0	"	8-10

From the above trials, it will be seen that these coals are all of excellent quality, and much on the same footing as steam-producers. It is to be regretted that the various companies do not have a systematic trial made of the evaporative powers of their coals, as they would undoubtedly, when reduced to the standard test of pounds of water evaporated from 212° F. per pound of coal burnt, give results at least equal to those from any bituminous coals burned in ordinary practice.

The Pictou Coal has been largely burnt on Atlantic and other steamers, and in this connection its firmness and non-liability to break up by handling, add materially to its value. Coals from this district afford a good, non-sulphurous coke, and possess the rare qualification of being adapted for use in blast furnaces in the raw state, and are well suited for mill work.

The Pictou coal is well prepared in various dimensions for domestic purposes, and the nut size from the Vale and Acadia Collieries, and the Deep Seam of the Halifax Co., is found suitable for use in soft coal base burners.

There are at present four companies working in this district. Their Collieries are large, and well equipped, and equal to an annual out-put of from 75,000 to 250,000 tons of coal. Details of the Collieries, their engines, styles of working, etc., will be found in the Reports of the Department of Mines.

There are within the limits of the Coal Field several large and valuable undeveloped areas; and in the event of an extension of trade, the out-put of the district could be very largely increased.

No complete estimate has yet been made of the coal contents of this district, as there is so large a portion of it untested. An idea of the immense quantity of coal contained by the thick seams of the Pictou Coal Field in a limited space, may be gathered from the fact that the area of the Halifax Company is estimated to contain 67,365,000 tons of available coal, after making every deduction for faults, lost pillars, etc.

The northern extension of this coal field is cut off at New Glasgow by a bed of conglomerate, believed to have been brought up by a fault from the upper part of the millstone grit.

This is succeeded to the north, in the district between New Glasgow and Pictou, by the upper, non-productive carboniferous measures. It is the opinion of Dr. Dawson and others, that the true coal measures are beneath this covering of new strata. Attempts were made to prove this by a borehole some years ago, but the operation was not carried far enough to allow of a decision. The truth of the opinion, which certainly is based on good grounds, should be carefully tested. If the anticipations prove correct, an immense coal field would be opened up under and around Pictou Harbor, the value of which could scarcely be estimated.

CUMBERLAND COAL FIELD.

This important County has only recently begun to take its place among the coal-producing districts. The first openings were made at the Joggins by the General Mining Association on two seams 4 and 6 feet thick. Operations have been conducted here for a number of years.

The coal has been extensively sold in St. John and other Bay of Fundy ports, as a house and steam coal.

The extension of these seams inland forms what is considered the northern edge of the coal field, and openings have been made at several points, on seams considered their equivalents. The identification of the seams, however, is not yet settled, as the continuity of the measures is broken by faults, and the beds themselves vary considerably.

At the River Hebert, a five foot seam has been opened, holding two partings, 16 and 10 inches thick, of shale. At Maccan, only two seams have been found of workable size, the lower being 4 ft. 4 in. thick, and the upper, 2 ft. 4 in.

At the Scotia and Cumberland properties, a seam is worked, which is by some supposed to represent a horizon lower than that containing the seams already noticed, and has the following section, measured in the new tunnel in the Chignecto Works, viz.:

	Ft.	In.
Top Coal	3·	0
Shaley Coal and Slate	2·	0
Coal	1·	2
Shale	0·	4
Coal	1·	0
Shale	0·	0½
Coal	2·	0
	9	6½

The coal is burnt to some extent locally, and is well liked; and the tramway, built a number of years ago, has been repaired, so as to allow of shipment over the Intercolonial Railway, distant two miles from the Colliery.

The most easterly opening in this district is known as the Styles Mine. The coal here is 8 feet thick, with a shaley parting of 5 inches in the centre. The coal is reported to be of good quality, and well adapted for house use. From its appearance, it should prove suitable for gas making; but I am not aware of any tests having been made.

So far as I am aware, little or no work has been done to ascertain what number of seams exist in the coal measures in the eastern part of the northern edge of the Coal Field, operations having been confined to a few outcrops offering ready access to the coal beds noticed above.

The southerly dip of the Joggins Coal measures reverses, and small seams of coal are said to occur about 20 miles to the south. As yet, however, there has been no exploratory work done to settle, even approximately, their line of outcrop. It is to be hoped that the labors of the Geological Survey will afford the necessary general information, which should precede, and not follow, the practical labors of the coal prospector, and that inducements will be held out sufficiently encouraging to warrant search for workable coal beds.

From the shore to Springhill little is known of the geological conditions of the country. The presence of woods, depth of soil, and small demand for coal, has prevented a search in a promising district, for a mineral of comparatively small value at the present moment, in in view of the extensive deposits already opened.

The following analyses will show the nature of the coal worked on the northern edge of the Field:

Composition.	Joggins.	Maccan.	Styles.	
			I.	II.
Moisture	2·50	....	4·05	3·72
Vol: Com: Matter, Fast Coking	....	....	38·18	37·66
Fixed Carbon, "	....	....	51·37	47·73
Vol: Com: Matter, Slow Coking	36·30	37·000	33·72	33·24
Fixed Carbon, "	56·00	59·174	55·83	52·15
Ash	5·00	3·826	6·40	10·89

At Springhill the coal seams have been extensively worked by the Springhill Coal Co., of St. John. Here the following section occurs:

	Ft. In.	Ft. In.
Seam	13.0	....
Strata	....	105.0
Seam	6.0	....
do.	....	130.0
Seam	2.4	....
do.	....	185.0
Main or North Seam	11·0	....
do.	....	80.0 (?)
South Seam	11·0	....
do.	....	100.0
Seam	2.6	....
do.	....	190.0
Seam	4.0	....
do.	....	176.0
Seam	2.9	....

Openings have been made on the Main and South Seams, and the coal has been found well adapted for house and steam purposes. Through the kindness of W. Hall, Esq., Manager of the Colliery, I am enabled to present the following full set of analyses of the Main or Black Seam, made by me some time ago: *

Main or Black Seam, 11 feet thick.

Composition.	Band No. 1.	No. 2.	No. 3.	No. 4.	No. 5.	No. 6.	No. 7.	No. 8.	No. 9.
Moisture	·96	·76	1·21	·30	·63	·90	1·34	·56	·41
Vol: Comb: Matter, Slow Coking	30·84	32·22	33·81	29·19	28·90	34·56	33·64	30·27	28·54
" " " Fast "	34·75	36·12	37·25	32·66	33·84	35·17	35·64	33·88	30·47
Fixed Carbon, Slow Coking	60·73	60·91	63·13	67·95	65·16	60·59	59·86	60·89	63·63
" " Fast "	57·82	57·01	59·69	64·48	60·22	59·98	57·56	57·28	61·70
Ash	7·45	6·11	1·85	2·56	5·31	3·95	5·16	8·28	7·42
Sulphur	·85	·56	·79	1·21	1·85	·89	1·40	2·65	2·25
Spec: Gravity	1·31	1·30	1·28	1·27	1·29	1·28	1·29	1·33	1·32
Theo: Evap: Power, Slow Coking	8·33	8·40	8·65	9·28	8·92	8·32	8·20	8·35	8·99
" " " Fast "	7·95	7·65	8·20	8·83	8·30	8·20	7·88	7·75	8·54

* See paper on "Canadian Coals," already referred to.

The following ultimate analysis of the coal is by Dr. Percy:

Carbon	78·51
Hydrogen	5·19
Oxygen, Nitrogen,	9·98
Sulphur	1·12
Ash	5·20

The coal of the overlying six foot seam presents the following composition, from an analysis by H. How, Jr.:

Ordinary Coking (air dry specimen) from outcrop—

Hygroscopic Moisture	3·47
Volatile Combustible Matter	26·98
Fixed Carbon	64·48
Ash	5·07
	100·00

Theoretical Evaporative power, 8·859 ℔s.; Sulphur, ·231; Specific Gravity, 1·30. The coal is compact, bright and clean, with conchoidal fracture.

On going eastward from Springhill the measures turn gradually to the north, but have not been opened on in this direction. Near Salt Springs Station a number of 3 feet seams have been found dipping about north, but have not yet been connected with those at Springhill. The country between this and the Styles Mine has not yet been proved, or, indeed, even prospected. Valuable discoveries may be anticipated, as the eastern edge of the basin is still unknown.

It will be seen that at present the area of this coal field is not ascertainable with precision; but, from the data available, it may be put down at 300 square miles. In the country extending along the head waters of the Waterford and Wallace Rivers and the Tatamagouche district to River John, embracing an area of some 500 square miles, the measures of the upper coal formation appear. It may be considered presumptuous to make such a statement at present; but when the extent of the coal now worked in England, in localities where at the surface newer rocks alone appear, is remembered, it is not unreasonable to predict that the district mentioned may prove very valuable. Should these upper or non-productive coal measures not be too thick, or should they allow the outcrop of the productive strata, there may be yet a coal district opened here equal in area to the sum of those now proved.

Seams of coal, up to three feet in thickness, have been found in this district; but hitherto no geological survey has determined the thickness or mapped out the extent of the covering rocks, nor have the investigations into the seams known to exist been systematically conducted.

I may remark that this point is well worthy the attention of the Canadian Geological Survey, and may very properly form a continuation of their work in the Cumberland district. Such an investigation carried into the district already mentioned, between Pictou and New Glasgow, would materially aid a decision, and afford data for renewing the investigation in a locality where its feasibility became recognised before the outlines of the geological relations in Cumberland and Colchester Counties were understood.

This County labors under the disadvantage of being, in some respects, not so near shipping places as Pictou and Cape Breton.

At present the Springhill Mines ship both at Dorchester and Parrsboro. The latter port is distant about 25 miles from the Mines, but offers the advantage of having not more than six to eight weeks of interrupted shipping; and a regularly established business would secure moderate freights to St. John and American towns.

Should the contemplated Railway from Springhill to Pugwash be built, an outlet would be made for shipments to Quebec and Montreal, by water; and the slack coal could be utilised for burning the large limestone deposits at Pugwash, for export to Prince Edward Island and the River St. Lawrence.

There was at one time a considerable quantity of coal shipped on the Maccan and Hebert Rivers; but, as an extra freight is demanded, on account of the shifting nature of the river channels, future shipments will probably be made at Sackville and Dorchester.

I have now briefly shown the extent of the various coal-producing districts, and presented a set of analyses, which, though not pretending to greater accuracy than those already familiar to the public, afford a better means of comparison between the various coals, as they were all made on a uniform system.

In conclusion, I would merely mention the extent of our coal resources. The known productive coal fields of the Province occupy an area of about 685 square miles, of which the Sydney and Cumberland fields comprise 600 miles; the remainder being divided between the Pictou, and the smaller coal fields of Antigonish and Cape Breton.

The area of the Province occupied by the upper coal measures has never been mapped with sufficient accuracy to allow of any estimate of its extent. I have already alluded to it, when speaking of the Pictou and Cumberland coal fields; and would add that, although we now have apparently more coal than required for our immediate wants, the discovery of coal in these districts, close to the water, would facilitate immensely our opportunities of supplying coal to the western parts of the Dominion. And any development of workable seams in the Shubenacadie district to which Dr. Dawson has drawn attention, would, from its close proximity to Halifax, allow of a cheap all winter shipment of coal, and furnish supplies of fuel, at a moderate cost, to the manufacturers of Halifax.

At many other localities discoveries of coal have been made; but the seams hitherto have not been considered of economic value. Among these may be mentioned the North River of Truro, and the Folly Mountain, where the opposing crops of a 20 inch seam, of fair quality, have been tested. "The outcrops of seams, varying from one to two feet in thickness, have been found at several places along the base of the Cobequids as far as Cape Chignecto. Indications of coal have also been observed in the coal measures band extending from Lower Stewiacke toward and along the Kennetcook River. These measures are not well exposed; and I believe nothing definite is known of their value. The occurrence of coal in this central district would, however, be of so great importance to the Province, and to the main line of Railway, that the subject well merits a thorough investigation."*

At Hunter's Mountain, near Baddeck, Loch Lomond, Salmon, and Gaspereaux Rivers, Neil's Cove, and many other localities in Cape Breton, the outcrops of small seams have been found, in carboniferous measures underlying the productive strata; but are not regarded, so far as explorations have been carried, as likely to prove valuable.

Petroleum.—The great oil reservoirs of this continent belong approximately to the Devonian and Lower Carboniferous measures. In this Province the latter system, wherever recognized, has been so much disturbed and metamorphosed that its yield of oil is, perhaps, problematical.

Indications of oil have been observed at Cheverie, Hants Co., permeating the gypsum and limestone of that locality, and are believed to have risen from underlying bituminous shales.

---

* Dawson's "Acadia Geology," p. 276.

At Lake Anslie, in Cape Breton, indications of oil have been observed in strata considered of the same age, and numerous attempts have been made to strike it by boreholes.

Numerous practical oil men have pronounced the signs, etc., indicative of extensive deposits; and a large expenditure is now being made, which will, it is to be hoped, prove successful.

CHAPTER II.

METALS AND THEIR ORES.— GOLD.— IRON.— COPPER.— LEAD.— SILVER.— ZINC.—ANTIMONY.—TIN.—MOLYBDENUM.—NICKEL AND COBALT.

THE GOLD FIELDS OF NOVA SCOTIA.

The Atlantic coast of Nova Scotia, from Canso to Yarmouth, is occupied by a series of measures presenting a rough, undulatory surface, diversified by numerous lakes and rivers, and arms of the sea running far into the land. The width of this district varies from 10 to 40 miles, and its area may be approximated at 6,500 square miles.

In this district are large belts of rock, commonly called granite, the limits of which have not yet been defined; but it is believed to form an irregular band, extending in a curve from Sambro to Cape Sable, and to form another interrupted belt, running from Waverley to Cape Canso. These bands are estimated by Prof. Hynd to cover about one-half of the district described above.

In the following description I have availed myself of all imformation, private and official, that I have had access to, and may mention, among the reconnaisance reports, those of Messrs. Poole, Campbell, Sterry Hunt, Selwyn, Heatherington, and Dr. Dawson, Prof. Hynd's detailed surveys of several districts, made to the Government, the Reports of the Department of Mines, etc.

Mr. Selwyn remarks that the Gold-bearing series in Nova Scotia closely resembles the Cambrian and Lingula flag series of North Wales, also auriferous. The lower members of both series, in both countries, consist of a succession of thick, bedded, greenish-gray, feldspathic grits and sandstones, or quartzites, with intercalated bands of shale; and these are similiarly overlaid comformably by black, earthy pyritous slates and sandy beds. On the south-west shore measures occur, as near Yarmouth, apparently belonging to the Quebec Group.

Mr. Poole, ex-Inspector of Mines, who has had extensive opportunities for observation, divides the former of Mr. Selwyn's divisions into two series, the lower consisting of slates and grits, crumpled, contorted, and cleaved transversely to the laminæ and holding lodes, not yet found productive. In the next series quartzites predominate, and productive lodes occur.

These measures are all metamorphosed, and especially so at certain points, as at Cochran's Hill, Sherbrooke district, where the slates have become steatitic, or talcose shists with rutile, garnets, etc.

This great series of strata has been thrown into well-defined east and west undulations, and again disturbed by a transverse series of undulations. The elevated points of intersection of these forces having been denuded, the lodes of gold-bearing quartz occur as sets of irregular ellipses. Prof. Whitney notices a similar connection of Californian lodes, with eroded anticlinals; and a corresponding arrangement has been observed in the Black Hills.

The lodes present white, vitreous, opaque or milky quartz, differing very much in color and structure, according to the varying conditions under which it is found. At Renfrew, it sometimes occurs crystallised, and showing banded vein structure, or holding pieces of slate, etc. The lodes contain, as accessory minerals, arsenides and sulphides of iron and lead, blende, copper pyrites, oxide of iron, copper glance, molybdenite, native copper, sulphur, chlorite, feldspar, garnets, mica, calcite, felsite, etc.; not, however, in quantities of economic importance.

Some lodes are apparently destitute of mineral matter, and hold but traces of gold. These are usually white and massive, vitreous to grannular, and occur sometimes fifteen feet in thickness.

The thinnest single lode worked is, perhaps, the Irving, at Mooseland, which varied in thickness from one-eighth to one-quarter of an inch. A lode 20 inches thick is considered a large one.

The gold occurs in the lodes in spots and bunches of the free metal, of every shape and size, up to 60 ounce nuggets. It is also present in the accompanying metals, as fine scales among their layers and crystals. I have not seen it reported in combination with Tellurium in this Province. It is stated to occur crystallised. Among some specimens Fifteen Mile Stream, I noticed one apparently a pseudomorph after a crystal of cubic pyrites one-fourth of an inch square.

The precious metal is not confined to the lode; for in both slate and quartzite walls, crevices have been found, holding gold, and but little quartz. Frequently where there are two or more lodes in slate, it is found profitable to crush the intervening slate also, which holds gold in laminæ, and in the almost omnipresent mispeckel. The occurrence of gold in cross lodes and leaders will be noticed further on.

The quartzite forming the hanging wall of some lodes has also been seen to hold fine gold close to the lode.

The age of the beds holding the auriferous lodes of the Province is not yet determined. Geologically speaking, they remain, in spite of many ingenious speculations, an unknown land. At first they were regarded as middle or lower Silurian; afterwards as Laurentian. At present, adopting the provisional divisions of the Geological Survey, they are considered of Cambrian age.

The ages of these rocks, unfortunately, cannot be determined by the imperfect and ill-preserved fossils that have been found. Their mineralogical characteristics are not to be relied upon for such a classification, as the strata cannot be traced into connection with any supposed counterparts on this continent. Their age can be approximated only by a systematic survey, which would require to be carried over the whole district in question. Although the age of these measures and the associated crystalline rocks is an interesting question, and, in some respects, a matter of practical importance, the survey would serve other most necessary purposes, commending it to all who are in any way connected with gold mining.

Our gold districts, as at present known, were the results of chance discoveries, and were generally found through boulders or exposures in brooks, etc. When it is considered that the worked area of many of the districts is very small, it strikes the mind of even the most casual observer that in the woods and swamps of the interior there must be many auriferous districts yet unknown. A geological survey which will map out all the axes of the undulations, the faults and their effects, their relation to the granites, etc., would be a great boon to the intelligent miner. By such a survey, certain lines would be found to present places where auriferous lodes would occur; for it is apparent that a general rule must apply to the production of similar districts over so extensive a range of country.

With such a map before him, the prospector could go at once to places where his labours would have a chance of success; and a systematic search would reveal many new districts. Our knowledge of the structure of the Gold Fields is lamentably deficient, and its elucidation would be considered a great aid to labor and capital ; and undoubtedly prove a source of increased revenue to the Province.

The Dominion Survey has not yet reached the Gold Fields; although I believe it was intended, some ten years ago, that they should be mapped out. The Province has done nothing beyond publishing reports on several districts, made for the Department of Mines by Prof. Hynd. It is true that the Dominion Survey has already given us a fair share of attention, when it is remembered that its appropriation for the enormous district extending from Cape Breton to Hudson's Bay and Vancouver's Island is no larger than that paid to the Geological Survey of the State of New York. But if it is found that they are unable to undertake it at present, I venture to suggest that a small annual grant might induce them to increase their staff in Nova Scotia. The survey would thus be made at the least expense to the Province, and be benefitted by the experience and resources of the Dominion department.

The money granted would be repaid by the possession of the topographical maps of the district under consideration, which would necessarily form part of the field work.

Such a survey would also prove another most important point, the neglect or non-trial of which has, it is to be feared, caused a permanent injury to many districts: That is, the question of the depth to which the lodes hold gold in paying quantity. Taking Tangier at the sea level, and Mount Uniacke 560 feet above the sea, we are ignorant at the present moment what relative line they mark in the downward extension of the lodes. The amount of denudation being unknown, it cannot be said which is the highest. It may be found that our Gold districts represent, as it were, steps in a ladder, whose length agrees with the estimated thickness of the auriferous series, some 3000 feet.

If such is the case, then the question of the auriferous quality of our lodes in depth would be affirmatively proved in a most satisfactory manner ; and the information gained outweigh many times the cost of the survey.

An important point in connection with the lodes is the question— are they beds or true veins ? The former view has been advanced by Dr. Sterry Hunt, Prof. Hynd, and others, who consider them similar to the Virginia and North Carolina deposits, as described by Profs. Silliman and Emmons.

Mr. Selwyn, the Director of the Dominion Geological Survey, who has had extensive experience in the Australian Gold Fields, considers them true veins; his reasons, which are clearly and concisely expressed, are to be found in G. S. R. 1870-71, p. 264. This view is supported by Mr. Poole (Report Dept. of Mines, 1878), who gives copious notes from a close observation, extending over a number of years.

His remarks are practical, and I give the following extract from the report, which is well worth perusal:

"Mining operations are not confined to the bedded leads, for rich streaks of paying quartz have been followed in cross leads and in what are called "angling" leads. As a rule true cross leads of later age than the true leads are barren, or contain but a few pennyweights of gold. Their influence, or that rather of some so-called cross leads, on the productiveness of a regular lead, is often remarked on, but cross-courses of later date are not always distinguished from contemporaneous connecting bands of quartz filling transverse fractures of the same age as the bedded leads. The effect of cross leads on the productiveness of regular leads is worthy of note. For instance, at the junction of a cross lead with the Belt lead at Montague, some rich spots gave as high as 40 ounces to the ton."

"In sections where slates predominate, and there are few alternating beds of quartzite, the leads are almost invariably barren, or so sparsely spotted as to be unprofitable to work."

"Angling leads are met, which cross the quartzites abruptly, and the slates gradually, proving rich in various instances in one or the other of the containing rocks."

"Sooner or later, in the working of the regular leads, inequalities characteristic of veins are met with. Late operations at Waverley, in the east end of the Union lead, have shown the quartz to cease, while the fracture continues its regular course. The workings have also exposed a regular 'horse' of quartzite, and in one part of the foot-wall a roll of compact quartz eight feet wide, which in parts yielded handsomely. From the roll a number of strings of gold-bearing quartz were found to ramify in all directions into the foot-wall of quartzite. One spot immediately below this roll gave 90 ounces from a lot of 5 tons; other strings in the foot-wall yielded largely. At a fault in this lead, drussy cavities contained crystals of quartz, galena, calcite, and iron pyrites. To mention one other instance, the West Lake at Uniacke contained a pocket beneath a swell in the lead five feet wide, so rich hat one crushing of 13 tons yielded 234 ounces.

"There are yet other characters suggestive of true veins; often there is a narrow band of slate next the lead, which is called 'gouge,' on account of the ease with which it is extracted with a thin, long-pointed pick. Its fissile nature probably is due to disturbance at the time the lead was formed. Again, thin leads have been known to taper out, and what may be called their continuation to start in the side slate, and expand to the original thickness from beyond the termination of the quartz at first worked.

"While many of the gold-bearing leads are regular and persistent for hundreds of feet, and lie parallel with wonderful uniformity, a careful following shows local troubles. Breaks and dislocations of the strata are not uncommon ; and while many undoubtedly are of later age, some appear to be contemporaneous."

He adds, in conclusion :

"The distinctive features of the gold leads of Nova Scotia are their general conformability with the slate and quartzite beds and their regularity, suggesting that they are rather beds than veins. But there are characters that point to their being true veins in spite of these features, and they are the following. The roughness of the planes of contact between quartz and slate and quartzite ; the crushed state of the slate or gouge on some footwalls ; the irregularity of their mineral contents ; the terminations of the leads ; the effects of contemporary dislocations ; and the influence of stringers and off-shoots on the richness of the leads. Characters that, singly or collectively, it would be difficult to account for, associated with a stratified deposit."

The experience of all the miners, both native and from Australia and the Western States, is united in calling the lodes true veins.

Although it may not be difficult to show that most auriferous quartz deposits are of later date than the enclosing rock, it is seldom possible to determine exactly the period of their formation. In this Province, however, the presence of Gold in a Lower Carboniferous Conglomerate at Gay's River, would show that some of the veins at least are of pre-Carboniferous age. On the other hand, there is no reason why other veins in the Province may not be even of Tertiary date, or immediately preceding the formation of the auriferous alluvions. This repeated or continuous formation of auriferous lodes has been noticed in other Countries.

ALLUVIAL GOLD.

Alluvial gold mining has not been carried on in Nova Scotia in any degree commensurate with the value of the auriferous deposits which are in a greater or less degree known to exist, and which, in all probability, occur to a much larger extent than is generally supposed.

An impression has arisen that the greater part of the gold districts of Nova Scotia, present nothing but rocky, denuded areas, without any, or at least very small, drift deposits. The contrary is, indeed, the case in some districts; and numerous wide spread surfaces exist where alluvial gold mining cannot fail to be pursued with great profit, if sufficient capital is embarked in the enterprise.

Drift deposits are found at Waverley, upwards of fifty feet deep ; and at Tangier similar deposits exist, which have already yielded remarkable returns, and have been abandoned on account of want of means to cope with the influx of water.

A moment's reflection will satisfy the most incredulous that, where rich Gold-bearing lodes are exposed near the surface, in the valleys adjacent to such exposures, or in crevices in the rocky surfaces, the gold from the denuded lodes must have accumulated by its gravity. When, however, the lodes occur at the summit of a hill or on its slope, much of the liberated gold will be found on the bed rock and in the crevices, or in the lowest stratum of drift, in the valley below, whether occupied by a lake, swamp, or by drift. It has been alleged that the greater part of the former auriferous drift of Nova Scotia has been carried by recent denuding action into the Atlantic, and now forms the sub-marine banks of the coast.

This has certainly no foundation, and Mr. Selwyn states, "I can confidently assert that bare rock surfaces are not more prevalent in the gold districts of Nova Scotia than they are in similar districts in Australia."

It is incredible that in the latter country, the Gold-bearing veins should be invariably accompanied by rich alluvial deposits; while in Nova Scotia the detrital deposits, which certainly occur under precisely similar conditions, should be almost as invariably unproductive. I do not believe in any such anomaly; but think the whole secret of the matter lies in the fact, that they have never yet been sought for with that degree of enterprise, intelligence, and preseverance which the investigation demands.

Tangier, Oldham, Sherbrooke, Waverley, Renfrew, and many other places, present all the conditions for alluvial diggings, both in the form of old channels and their re-worked condition.

Having briefly noticed the lodes, their nature, contents and associated rocks, the various districts next claim attention. It would take up far too much room, were I to submit anything approaching a detailed account of each one, and such description would necessarily be imperfect; for during the last few years operations in many of them have been carried on chiefly by tributors in a very desultory manner.

I will, with your permission, give the position of each district, and a notice of any peculiarities of the lodes, their contents, value, etc.

Carribou.—This district is situated 6 miles south of the Musquodoboit River, at Hamilton's Corner, about 36 miles from the Shubenacadie Station, from which point a tri-weekly mail runs to the Mines. Work of a preparatory character was undertaken first in 1867, I believe, and has been carried on in an intermittent manner ever since. Several of the lodes have paid well, as the North, Flat, Cross, and Hyde Lodes; of which the Cross Lode, at one time, gave quartz carrying 20 oz. A lode on the Bushing Area was found to lie for some distance in a horizontal position, apparently in the summit of an anticlinal. In 1877, a lode, found on Area 629, Block 2, one foot thick, yielded, in 6 months, 1170 oz., from a stope of 40 feet, and within a depth of 120 feet, the shoot of rich quartz being vertical, and at the junction of a cross lode.

Moose River.—This district lies about 7 miles west of Carribou, and is accessible by a road from Middle Musquodoboit; and has only recently received attention. The surface is reported to carry Gold, but the attempts made to wash it, proved unsuccessful, it is reported, from improper construction of the flume. Several promising lodes and many rich boulders have been found; and it is stated that in Dec., 1879, Henry Archibald had discovered a lode yielding over two oz. to the ton.

Fifteen Mile Stream.—This district lies on a tributary of the East River of Sheet Harbor, about 19 miles from the head of navigation. It is very inaccessible, there being no carriage-road to it. Explorations have been carried on here for several years, and have shown the presence of a large number of promising lodes; and two crushers were built. Its isolation, and the expense of getting supplies, have retarded the opening of this district, which, however, is again receiving attention.

Gay's River.—This district is an interesting one, although it has never occupied an important position as far as its yield of Gold is concerned. It is situated about 6 miles east of Shubenacadie Station, on a tributary of Gay's River. Here the gold slates are overlaid by flat beds of carboniferous conglomerate, an ancient consolidated drift. The Gold occurs in grains and scales at the base of the conglomerate, and in backs in the slates; small auriferous lodes have also been observed in the slates. The modern drift overlying the conglomerate has also yielded Gold, derived from a similar source, or from the natural working over of the conglomerate. The mining has been done by levels, driven in the conglomerate at the junction of the two formations; but no rule has yet been observed indicating the position of the Gold.

Lawrencetown.—This district lies about 12 miles east of Halifax Harbor. In the early days of mining here, a considerable quantity of Gold was taken from rich boulders and washings. The chief vein on the Werner property was 8 inches thick, of bluish quartz, showing gold, blende and mispickel. The Capel Townsend property embraces several groups of Gold-bearing veins; that known as the Waddilow group includes thirteen. The quartz, generally enclosed in slates, is somewhat ferruginous, and contained copper pyrites, blende, and a little galena. Some of these lodes were reported to have yielded well. Operations, however, have been almost totally suspended, after large sums had been spent in preparatory work, mills and machinery. The mining that has been done of late years has been confined chiefly to Crookes' lode, the first opened; and it yielded well at the junction of cross veins.

A large number of promising lodes are known here, and there is no reason why they should not be worked profitably; and it is to be hoped that another and more successful start will soon be made.

Montagu.—This district lies about 6 miles east of Dartmouth, near Lake Loon, and has maintained an average out-put for a number of years, greatly increased during 1870 and the three following years. The best known lodes are, perhaps, the Belt, Werner, St. Patrick, and Cross Veins.

The Belt lode has been worked by several parties, and notably, by the Messrs. Lawson, who, in the five years ending with 1874, extracted about 10,000 ounces, with a handsome profit. The lode is enclosed in slate, separating it from quartzite, and varies in thickness from 4 to 20 inches. The quartz is highly crystalline, and shows, besides Gold, iron and copper pyrites, and mispickel. The sesulphurets, according to Prof. Silliman, are most abundant near the underlying slate, which also holds gold and mispickel in lumps, sometimes weighing 50 ℔s.

During the tenancy of the Messrs. Lawson, a plan was kept, showing the milling value of each parcel of quartz extracted. This plan, while showing how irregularly the Gold is distributed in the vein, also determines the extent and character of the Gold streak. The richest part of the lode at the surface was at the Main shaft; in depth it trended to the westward.

For many years, the presence of rich boulders in the surface cover of the eastern part of the district, caused the expenditure of much time and money in a search for the parent lode. In the Spring of 1879, Mr. G. Stuart, and his associates, found the vein, called from the colour of the quartz, the Rose Lode. It varies in thickness from 4 to 18 inches; as yet the workings on it are limited, but enough has been done to show a very rich chimney, dipping westward, at an angle of 30°.

Up to the present date 292 tons have been crushed, yielding 1086 oz. The property has been purchased by American capitalists, who have removed the steam mill, built by Mr. Lawson, and considered one of the best in the province, from the Belt Lode, to the new shaft, where it will also do duty as a pumping and winding engine. It is to be hoped that their success will draw attention to the district, and lead to fresh discoveries. During the past year, a lode close to the Symonds Mill yielded well at the junction of numerous cross veins, and promises to become more valuable than even the Rose Lode.

Waverley.—This district lies about 3 miles east of Windsor Junction Station, on the Intercolonial Railway. It has been reported on by Prof. Hynd, in 1869, and a full description given, which is too long for re-production here. I am not aware of any developments since the date of his report, which are calculated to throw any fresh light on the structure of the district. In the year 1865, the returns gave a produce of 14,000 oz., but the annual out-put has since dwindled away to a few hundred ounces.

Among the chief lodes that have been worked, may be mentioned the Tudor, Brodie, South, and Taylor veins. Large and extensive works were carried on by Mr. Burkner, the DeWolf Co., the Boston and other Companies, but they gradually ceased working, as the main leads became impoverished at depth, and varying from 150 to 400 feet. Since that date, operations have been carried on chiefly by individuals and tributors, who have taken out blocks left by the previous workers, and extracted quartz from new lodes. Some of these new veins have yielded fairly, as the United, American Hill, New South, the No. 6 Lode.

The barrel quartz, in the eastern part of the field, attracted much curiosity at one time. Here the lodes follow the strata, as they bend over in an anticline. The corrugations generally present the form of wave-like undulations, rarely that of tight folds, and at one place, a little to the westward, one of the lodes presents a nearly horizontal sheet. The quartz is somewhat banded, and holds calcite, apparently of later date, filling fissures in the lode. This has been worked at intervals for a number of years, and is said to have averaged 12 dwts. to the ton.

Oldham.—This Gold Field is situated 3 miles east of Enfield Station. Gold was discovered here in 1861, and since that date operations have been carried on, with occasional periods of depression.

The worked portion of the district is characterized by a valley, having a nearly east and west course, occupying the crown of a very sharp anticlinal fold, the axis of which is nearly parallel to the area lines.

From records obtained by Prof. Hynd, it appears that in this district the pay streak dips east, generally at a low angle.

Among the most noticiable lodes, are the Barrel, Ohio, Frankfort, Ritchie, Hall, Britannia, etc. A large amount of gold was extracted in 1877, by Mr. Baker, from a lode on the eastern turn of the measures, the result of five months work being 1,280 oz. On areas 101 to 105 the Blackie lode was worked for some time in search of the mispickel nodules, which were found to carry gold up to 5 and 7 ozs., per ton.

Messrs. Donaldson have worked extensively on the Britannia, Hall, and other lodes, on the north side of the district. Mention has already been made of the "Angling Lodes," of which interesting examples occur here.

The low angle of dip of the pay streak has probably been the cause of the comparatively shallow character of the workings carried on here, which proves an impediment to systematic mining.

This is to be regretted, as preliminary labours carried on in common would have facilitated operations, and the work, so far as it has been carried, proves that the district promises to be one of unusual richness.

Renfrew.—This district lies about 7 miles west of Enfield Station, near the north end of Grand Lake. Work was begun here about the same time as at Oldham, and the returns show a steady increase to 7,904 oz., in 1867 ; and a decrease to but 3 ozs., in 1874 ; since that date there has been a slight improvement. Among the more prominent lodes may be named, the Preeper, Sims, North, South and Brook.

The operations of the Ophir Company were systematically conducted for several years, and handsome profits realized, but workings, were abandoned at a depth of 350 feet. Their returns during five years were 17,532 ozs., 13 dwt. 21 gr. from 21,012 tons of quartz.

All the mining has hitherto been confined to the south side of the anticlinal ; the measures on the north side are generally covered by soil, and although rich boulders have been found, the parent lodes remain for future workers.

The proximity of lower carboniferous measures and their position relative to the lodes, furnish, according to Prof. Hynd's report, favourable conditions for the accumulation of alluvial gold.

Sherbrooke.—This district lies about 38 miles by stage from Antigonish, on the Halifax and Cape Breton Railway, near the village of Sherbrooke, on the St. Mary River, and ranks first in the list of the Provincial Gold Fields.

Up to September, 1866, this district produced 19,101 ozs., at the rate of 1 oz., 16 dwt. to the ton. In the following year, 5,809 tons yielded 8,522 ounces of gold.

The lodes and associated rocks present no features distinguishing them from those of other localities in the Province.

Among the numerous operations, the Wellington may be mentioned. Here work has been carried on ever since the discovery of gold in the district. The Wellington, Dewar, and other veins have been mined to depths varying from 400 to 600 feet. The proprietors have conducted their operations with care and prudence, and received a good return. Between the years 1863 and 1869, they extracted 8,984 tons, which yielded 12,215 ozs., and similar results have since been obtained. On the adjoining Grapevine properties, favourable returns have been made for a number of years.

Other properties yielded well, but are now chiefly let on tribute. Among those that have paid well during the past year may be mentioned the Dominion, worked by Messrs. Fraser & Bent, and the Wentworth, under lease to Mr. Hattie. A very large amount of work has been done by other parties in this district, and it appears, from the continual discovery of workable lodes, likely to afford equally encouraging results for a long time to come.

At Cochran's Hill, in this District, a little work has been done in lodes running in slate belts, and also at the Crow's Nest, two miles to the westward. The strata here, as already mentioned, are highly metamorphosed. The yield, so far, per ton, has been low, from 4 to 8 dwts.; but the cheapness of extraction has enabled work to be carried on at a profit.

Isaac's Harbor.—This district, known officially as Stormont, lies east of Sherbrooke. For several years the returns gave an annual yield of about 1400 oz.; but during the last few years the mines have remained almost entirely neglected. Promising lodes have been found in the surrounding country, but have not yet been thoroughly tested. No district in the Province has better promise for the future than the one now under consideration. The extent of mining that was carried on is very small, and limited to a few lodes. The Mulgrave lode yielded from two areas in 1863-4, 621 tons of quartz, giving 1897 ounces of Gold; and the little work done since has frequently yielded equally well.

Wine Harbor.—This district lies on the coast, about 4 miles east of the mouth of St. Mary's River, and 12 miles from Sherbrooke.

Here the auriferous quartz lodes are met with, over a belt nearly a mile from north to south, and are in thick bedded quartzites, generally associated with thin layers of finely laminated, bluish slate, which facilitates mining.

This district also shows, in its returns, the same falling off from the best year, 1864, when 4,033 ounces were obtained.

Work has been confined chiefly to the ground owned by the Eldorado Company, where it has been continued by tributors since the proprietors ceased operations. The property of the Provincial Company has frequently yielded good quartz, the Caledonia Company having mined in six months $200,000 of Gold. The Hattie lode has also yielded good returns to those who have worked it.

Tangier.—This district lies on the Atlantic shore, about fifty miles east of Halifax, from which town it can be reached by a tri-weekly mail, and is well known as the earliest opened. In the eastern part of the district, at Strawberry Hill, work has been pursued for a number of years, chiefly on lodes, known as the Dunbrack and Forrest, and others associated. The strata and the lodes are cut by a granitoid (?) dyke, about 15 feet wide, which can be traced for several miles in a southwest direction. It does not appear to affect the contents of the lodes in any way, nor to have shifted them.

A number of lodes extending to the Tangier River, have been worked at various times; among them may be mentioned the Feld, Leary, Nigger, etc., which have yielded fair returns in the moderate depth they have been worked to.

A considerable quantity of gold was found in the alluvion at one place in this district, and a pond called Copper Lake was partially drained. Prof. Silliman states that a layer of tough clay and glacial drift was found underneath the mud and vegetable matter, and everywhere in the under clay small unrounded nuggets were found. The work of washing was, however, abandoned, as the drainage was not carried deep enough to allow its proper application.

Mount Uniacke.—This Gold Field lies about 3 miles from Mount Uniacke Station, on the Windsor Railway. A large number of lodes have been exposed over an area having a breadth of about one and a half miles, and a length, it is said, of six miles. The veins are similar to those of other districts, and enclosed in quartzite, frequently with linings of slate. Their thickness varies from one inch to several feet, and the large veins are sometimes divided into layers by interlaminations of slate.

"The crystalline quartz, sometimes milky-white, sometimes bluish, the latter being often laminated, fills the greater part of the lodes, and generally the widest ; while arsenical iron pyrites, or mispickel, is, at the outcrop, the mineral of the narrower lodes. Certain quartz lodes appear to the sight almost entirely destitute of foreign matter, while others contain metallic sulphides, such as cubical iron-pyrites, often decomposed, mispickel, and, sometimes, blende, galena, and copper pyrites. I have observed in all the selvages of some lodes, a blackish earthy substance which appeared to me to be the oxide of manganese.

"A great irregularity of formation and of structure characterises generally the lodes in the area under review. One sees lodes hardly impregnated with arsenical iron-pyrites at the outcrop, in narrowing in depth, become converted into veinlets of pure mispickel. Such lodes measuring several inches at their outcrop, are reduced to a mere thread at a few feet in depth, while others are subject to successive and sudden contractions and swellings. But the most extraordinary case of irregularity, is that of the lodes which assume curiously twisted shapes by branching sometimes to the north, sometimes to the south. The constancy of formation and structure, that is to say, the regularity of the deposits, has been, so far, the rarest case with the lodes in these areas ; but experience has demonstrated in many localities, that the disorders which I have described, often disappear at a certain depth."—Rep. H. Y. Hynd.

The report, from which the above extract is taken, contains interesting information about the number, position and assays of the lodes, and their relation to the geological features of the surrounding country.

Among other districts, may be mentioned the Ovens in Lunenburg County, where alluvial washings were carried on for a short time ; Gold River, Yarmouth, Stewiacke, Chezzetcook, Ship Harbor, Harrigan Cove, Moose Head, Ecum Secum, etč. Gold has also been reported from the Cobequid and South Mountains.

In Cape Breton, the Middle River, Baddeck, was, some years ago, made a Gold district, under the name of Wagamatcook, but no profitable lodes have been found, although the slates occasionally yield scales of Gold, and it occurs everywhere in the beds of the streams. Mr. Campbell, in his report, in 1863, gives an interesting account of his examination of the northern part of Cape Breton, and reported alluvial Gold in the sands of many of the brooks.

The initiation of Gold mining in the Province, was by men but little skilled in mining; their operations consisted in trenches and shallow workings. The companies that next succeeded, opened veins on a large scale, built mills, etc., but in too many cases made no provision for those periods, common to the history of all fissure veins, when much expensive dead work is required.

At present, the mining is chiefly in the hands of men of comparatively small means, who, however, have gained practical experience, and their economy and care have frequently yielded them handsome returns.

Every visitor to the various districts, is struck by the want of system shown in the early workings. Long trenches following the outcrops, shallow pits, and lodes stoped to grass, all show a neglect of fundamental principles, costing succeeding miners much money. This state of affairs, which is common to the ineption of all mining operations, has, in Nova Scotia, been unfortunately perpetuated by the system of letting areas and lodes to two or three working miners, who pay a percentage royalty on the Gold they extract.

On this subject, Mr. Poole very properly remarks: Report Dept. of Mines, 1873.

" A complete change has taken place in the system of working the Gold mines, and with the change there has been a great falling off in the number of men engaged, and a consequent decrease in the yield of Gold. The change referred to, is the almost total discontinuance from operating by companies and the introduction of the system of working the mines by tribute.

"Two or more practical working miners agree among themselves to take a mine, often one that an agent for a Company has failed to work at a profit, for a term of six months or a year, with the understanding that they pay to the owners a percentage of the value of the Gold extracted.

" Already it is shown that some of the leads abandoned by Companies can, in the hands of tributors working even under many difficulties, be wrought with profit and advantage.

" The great objection to tributing, as now conducted, is the desultory method it introduces. The backs of the leads are stripped, and the trenches thus made, become reservoirs for water. No more timber than is absolutely necessary for the immediate safety of the mine, is, as a rule, used, and in districts where the country rock is fissile, a crushing in of the walls sooner or later takes place."

Again, in 1874 :

"In the last report, reference was made to the introduction of the tribute system of mining, by which working miners are enabled to utilize their knowledge and labour to the greatest advantage. It is, undoubtedly, the best adapted to foster a true mining spirit. As far as possible, it should be encouraged, and few official obstructions put in the way of working men willing to venture their labour in mining speculations. At the same time, it should not be forgotten that men of this class are almost always without the capital requisite to open the setts as thoroughly as even they themselves would approve of doing, had they adequate means; but for the supply of their immediate necessities, they are compelled to extract quartz as speedily as possible, and get some return for their labor. The system, as at present conducted, is only adapted for surface workings, and where the water is light. It is attended by this great disadvantage, that the tributers' interest in the property they work, being merely temporary, they leave the small shafts and slopes imperfectly stowed and secured, in consequence of which rupture of the walls sooner or later taking place, allows free access for the infiltration of surface water. This admission of water is not of so much importance when the depth of the workings is shallow, but most serious when great. In most cases it ultimately leads to abandonment, due either to the want of capital necessary to erect pumping apparatus, or because the expense incurred by pumping becomes insupportable. Unfortunately this country is comparatively level and wet, so that adits for unwatering a district can seldom be resorted to, and pumps have generally to be used. When mines have been abandoned and allowed to fill with water, much expense is entailed on the workers of leads in adjoining areas on account of the water, which finds its way down from the denuded outcrop and through the shattered rock. Were lessees to require proper attention to be paid to the protection of the outcroppings of the leads, either by requiring them to be left unwrought, or the excavated space be well packed, and the walls kept from falling together, much of this trouble might be avoided. The lessees could make such stipulations with the tributers, and their agent on the ground could see them carried out.

"Most of the claims are held in small areas, and while they are so, companies cannot work to advantage. Capital might, perchance, however, be profitably invested by being more particularly directed to supplying efficient machinery to do the hoisting and pumping, the leads so drained and made workable being divided into setts and worked by tributers, at rates proportionate to the value of the quartz previously extracted from each sett."

The lodes are opened by shafts sunk on their dip, at intervals of 50 to 150 feet. These are connected by levels, and the vein-containing rock opened by stopes, arranged to suit the number of men, proportion of dead rock, etc. The stoping is generally under-hand, or a combination of both systems, scaffolds being placed for convenient stowage. After the rock covering the lode has been removed for some distance, the lode which has been secured temporarily in its place, is removed at one operation, and passed directly to the mill.

The ore is hoisted and the pumps driven by every possible contrivance, from a steam engine to a wind-mill, and the mill engine is frequently employed for all these purposes. Few shafts have been sunk over 200 feet; the deepest being on the Wellington property, at Sherbrooke, which has reached over 500 feet. Dynamite is extensively used, and many hard bound lodes have been profitably worked by its application, which would otherwise have remained unattacked. As yet machine drills have not been used, they have proved awkward in the narrow workings, which seldom exceed 2 feet 6 inches in width, and are moreover inclined.

The distribution of the Gold in "pay streaks" is common to the quartz lodes of all countries; and is connected with some law, concerned in the original lines of openings and pressure, whereby the various minerals were deposited in the lodes; but, as yet, we are not in possession of the data for its practical application. In Nova Scotia, the dip varies from east to west, and each district has its own experience to guide the miners. It is to be regretted that no records or plans have been kept, for an accumulation of data would have proved most useful on this point. The streaks are found to vary in width, and sometimes to be lenticular, and to die out before coming to the surface. It thus happens that frequently the miner finds himself confronted by barren quartz, becomes discouraged, and abandons his work, when prospecting tunnels might have disclosed another streak at no great distance.

Dr. Sterry Hunt remarks:

"To abandon a working on account of a momentary impoverishment of the lode, as has too often been done in this region, is therefore unwise; and a large enterprise, where mining is carried on in several veins at a time, the richness of some of these may always be counted upon to compensate for the temporary poverty of others. I am of opinion that an unnecessary discouragement has had as much to do with the failure of certain Gold-mining enterprises in Nova Scotia as the want of scientific knowledge and the neglect of proper preparations, and that many of these now abandoned as unprofitable, *will be again taken up with advantage.*"—*Gold Regions of Nova Scotia.*—*Geo. Sur.*, 1866.

This subject leads to the consideration of permanence in depth of the Gold yield; in some districts it is considered that no Gold will be found in paying quantity, beyond a certain depth. This probably is a case of a pay streak lying in a comparatively horizontal position, and having an unproved interval of barren quartz below it.

The depth to which mining can be carried is so small when compared with the known thickness of the strata of the globe, and the distance through which the lode-forming agency has acted, that the work of the Nova Scotia miners appears but a scratch It will, undoubtedly, be found that there need be no apprehension of the limit of the latter in depth, being reached at distances less than those through which we know them, from surface evidence, to extend horizontally in directions parallel, and transverse to the anticlinal axes; and as these distances are reckoned by thousands of feet, it may very safely be conjectured that there is practically no limit to the depth to which the lodes may be successfully followed.

The quartz passes from the shafts to the mill dump, where it is sorted and broken by hand for the stamps. The mills are of the common pattern, with revolving stamps, weighing generally from 550 to 700 lbs.; although a few mills run with 450 lbs. stamps, working in cast iron boxes. The batteries are provided with tables, and in some cases with secondary oscillating plates, or tail runs, with or without ripples.

I believe the use of plates in the batteries has not been tried, at any rate, it is not in practice.

The mills generally comprise two or three batteries, of four or five stamps each, and are driven by steam or water, according to the facilities offered by the district. This influences the cost of crushing, which varies per ton from 90 cts., to $1.50 for water, and from $1.50 to $2.50 for steam mills.

The system of battery amalgamation is universally adopted; the use of blankets is unknown, and no attempts, beyond an occasional settling tub, are made to catch any lost amalgam, etc.

The methods outlined above, answer tolerably well, for much of the Nova Scotia Gold, which is present in a coarse, free form, but prove inadequate to treat fine Gold and that held in the pyrites. No regular system of assaying tailings and pyrites has ever been carried out here, but the tests made show what a shameful waste has gone on since gold mining began.

The following results, from Prof. Hynd's reports, will show this point; it being remembered that in practical working, these per-centages would seldom be realised:

Districts.	Per Ton.					
	Yield of Gold.			Yield of Silver.		
	Oz.	Dwts.	Grs.	Oz.	Dwts.	Grs.
WINE HARBOR. Assay of pure Arsenical Pyrites from Provincial Co....................	11	8	16	..	..	..
SHERBROOKE. Assay of pure Arsenical Pyrites and Galena from Boulder Lot....................	4	1	16	8	19	10

Continued.

District.	Per Ton.					
	Yield of Gold.			Yield of Silver.		
	Ozs.	Dwts.	Grs.	Ozs.	Dwts.	Grs.
Assay of pure Arsenical Pyrites (no Galena) from Cobourg Co..................	1	12	16	6	10	16
Assay of pure Arsenical Pyrites from Kingston and Sherbrooke Co............	4	18	..	5	14	8
Assay of pure Arsenical Pyrites from Canada Co................................	45	..	..	..	..	..
Assay of pure Arsenical Pyrites from Wentworth Co. (Ferguson lode)..........	..	16	8	..	..	..
Assay of pure Arsenical Pyrites from Meridian Co. (Sears lode)...............	1	12	16	9	..	..
Assay of Concentrated Tailings (average).....	2	10	..	..	..	..

TANGIER GOLD DISTRICT.

No. 1. Assay of pyrites from tailings at the mill of the New York and Nova Scotia Co., Tangier, made Sept. 23, 1863, by Dr. John Torrey, Assay Office, U. S.:

    Gold, per ton (of 2000 ℔s.).................... $122.13
    Silver 2.67
                                                               $124.80

No. 2. Pyrites from Lake Co's. lead, crushed at White and Esty's mill on the Tangier River. These assays were made January 14, 1865, by O. D. Allan, of Yale College.

    Mean of two assays gave:
        Gold, per ton (2000 ℔s.).......................$187.04

No. 3. Assay of pyrites from tailings of the Leary lode, made Dec. 31, 1863, by E. N. Kent, U. S. Assay Office, in New York:

    Gold, per ton (2000 ℔s.)..................... $93.05
    Mean of three assays:
        Gold, per ton (2000 ℔s.)..................... $134.99

WAVERLEY GOLD DISTRICT.

No. 1. One ton (2000 lbs.).............. $6.30
No. 2.   "   " 7.78
No. 3.   "   " 7.59

From five pounds of tailings (No. 2) all the silicious particles were washed out, leaving 3 oz. 11 dwts. of sulphurets, which gave 6 oz., 14 dwts. 1 gr. of gold, and 10 dwts. silver to the ton of 2000 lbs.

Mr. Burkner sent to Freiburg, 1st—850 lbs. of pyrites from cleanings in stamper boxes, in which quartz of $2\frac{1}{2}$ to 3 oz. per ton had been crushed; the assay return was $600 to the ton. 2nd. Two tons of pyrites from quartz from 15 dwts. to 20 dwts. to the ton, assay return $150 per ton. 3rd. 8 or 10 tons pyrites from tailings which gave $18 or $20 to the ton; the first and second lot of pyrites gave about as much quicksilver as gold.

"Assays made under my (Prof. B. Silliman) directions on the waste tailings from "barrel quartz," run through a stamping mill at Waverley, showed the presence of nearly fifteen pennyweights of gold to the ton of tailings, not over eight pennyweights having been saved in the original working."

The average amount of gold in the tailings, quartz, of our mills, may, according to Prof. Hynd and others, be averaged at 4 dwts. to the ton.

Mispickel from the O'Connor lode, at Montagu, gave $276.49 per ton of gold and silver. A ton of pyrites crushed at Montagu gave 37 ozs. of gold, and the tailings of the crush assayed 11 ozs.

The mean yield of two samples of tailings from Montagu quartz crushed at Waverley, gave Professor Silliman 16 dwts. 13 grs. gold per ton.

"A series of assays proved that the tailings taken from the bank close to the Montagu mill contained $37 per ton, and gradually decreased towards the furthest end of the heap, to $2.80 per ton. A natural concentration had here taken place—the heavier portions, consisting principally of pyrites carrying gold, had settled close to the mill, while the lighter portions, poor in gold, were carried by the water to a greater distance."

When it is considered that auriferous sulphurets are present in almost every lode worked, frequently in large proportions, and are also, in some districts, abundant in the enclosing rocks, there is evidently a field for profitable extraction of gold yet untouched.

It has been stated that at least 20 per cent. of the gold originally present in the lodes, is allowed to pass through the mills, and to escape to the nearest brook or pond, some mill owners boasting of their facilities for getting rid of the tailings.

It would be useless for me to repeat the advice that has been frequently offered on this point, or to bring forward the statistics of other countries as to the profitable treatment of pyrites, economy of milling, etc. ; but it certainly appears that a system of concentrating the sulphides, etc., and their subsequent treatment, would prove profitable.

Those who desire further information will find the subject treated of in Prof. Hynd's reports, the works of Śmyth, Phillips, Kustel, and others.

Nova Scotia Gold, like that of other countries, is an alloy in which silver forms the chief of the impurities. The following analyses will show its character:

Locality.	Authority.	Gold.	Silver.	Iron.	Cop'r.	Lead.	Zinc.	Total.
Old Tangier....................	O. C. Marsh.......	98·13	1·76	trace.	0·05	......	......	99·94
Tangier (Field Lode)...........	B. Silliman.......	97·25	2·75	......	......	......	......	100·00
" (Leary Lode)..........	U. S. Assay Office..	96·60	......	......	......	......	......	......
Waverley (Laidlaw's)..........	H. How	94·69	4·74	......	0·39	......	0·16	99·98
Ovens	A. Geener........	93·06	6·60	......	0·09	......	......	99·75

The average fineness of the gold from different countries is as follows

```
Victoria............................. 958 in 1000
Nova Scotia.......................... 955  "   "
Australia............................ 925  "   "
California........................... 880  "   "
Russia............................... 891  "   "
British Columbia..................... 875  "   "
```

When samples of gold from different mines, or even different mining districts, are taken, the variation is sometimes remarkable, and, owing to impurities introduced during the smelting operation, the bar gold is sometimes by no means as fine as the native alloy; but, by care in the manipulation, the fineness of many samples could be materially increased, and the character of the native gold at any particular mine sustained.

The character of the gold at any particular mine is of more importance than generally supposed. Gold from Tangier, for example, yielded to Marsh, 981 parts of gold in 1000 of the native alloy; whereas, gold from the Ovens gave the same assayist 920 parts to 1000, being a difference of 61 ounces in a thousand ounces of the metal.

The loss of weight in smelting the rough product of amalgamation varies from one to fourteen per cent. The value of the gold liable to pay Government royalty is estimated at the rate of nineteen dollars an ounce, troy, for the smelted, and eighteen dollars for the unsmelted metal.

In the preceding pages I have endeavored, as concisely as possible, to lay before you the extent of the country containing gold, as yet undeveloped and almost unprospected; and to show that in every district the careful miner has succeeded in his operations. The ground already worked, and affording space for still more extensive mining in the future, is very large, as will appear from the number and extent of the districts. The nature and contents of the veins and associated minerals have been shown by many writers and practical men to recall those of noted gold-yielding countries. From the returns, it will be seen that the average yield of our quartz, even when lessened by careless milling, and the neglect of the auriferous sulphurets, is higher than in almost any country mining quartz lodes. Practical miners from other countries are again turning their attention to our gold districts, and with the approved appliances of the past few years, such as strong explosives, drills, simpler pumps, revolutionised mill economies, it is to be hoped that judiciously expended capital will once more be invested in them. In every country, an apprenticeship in mining seems indispensable; and it may not be a premature hope, when so many years have thus been passed, that at last the necessity for conducting gold mining on business principles has been recognised here.

The tables given in the appendix will show the total returns of quartz crushed, yield of gold, men employed, etc.

THE IRON ORES OF NOVA SCOTIA.

This, the most important of our mineral resources, has not as yet received attention at all commensurate with its value. The ores, as will be seen from the following information, are of the most varied species; many of them of extreme purity. They are generally accessible, near water or Railway transport, and none of them at any great distance from coal.

The existence of the leading ore beds has been known for many years, and desultory attempts were made to work them in Annapolis and Pictou Counties. A description of the furnaces and of the causes which led to their abandonment will be found in Dr. Harrington's report on the Iron Ores of Canada, Geo. Sur. 1872-3.

In the following report, I have drawn largely on a paper on "Nova Scotia Iron Ores," which, accompanied by geological maps, was submitted by me to the North of England Institute of Mining Engineers, in 1876, and subsequently published in their Transactions. This I have supplemented by some analyses of my own, and information drawn from various official sources, so as to give the latest available details.

The geological ages, positions, extent, and qualities of the ores, are the chief points at present noticeable, the economic development being as yet so limited.

The geological range of the best-known ores will be readily seen from the following table:

GEOLOGICAL AGE.*	VARIETY OF ORE FOUND.
Modern....................	Bog ores. Iron ore Sand.
Triassic Trap...............	Magnetite. Red hematite.
CARBONIFEROUS { Upper coal measures........	Clay ironstone.
True coal measures..........	Clay ironstone.
Millstone grit..............	Spathic ore.
Lower Carboniferous marine formation	{ Clay ironstone, spathic, red hematite and limonite.
Lower coal measures........	
Devonian (Oriskany sandstone)....	Specular and magnetite.
Upper Silurian (Lower Helderberg)	Red hematite. Limonite.
Upper Silurian ?..............	{ Specular and magnetite of Pictou, Limonite of Londonderry.
Lower Silurian ?.............	Titaniferous and specular ore.
Laurentian ?................	Red hematite. Magnetite.

These ores form a broad band extending from end to end of the Province, and in the description, following the band from west to east, the ores will be noticed as they are successively met.

* The Geological ages are taken from the reports of the Geo: Sur:, and Dr. Dawson's Acadian Geology.

In the dykes and masses of trap associated with the Triassic sandstones of the south side of the Bay of Fundy, are numerous veins and pockets of magnetite and red hematite, as far as known, not exceeding in any case, one foot in thickness. The magnetite is generally very pure, the chief foreign ingredient being silica. It is usually massive, sometimes crystallised in dodecahedra and its combinations in partly filled veins, and associated with quartz, colourless and amethystine. Near Digby Neck, it is found with red hematite, and several hundred tons have been extracted for smelting.

The following analyses, by Dr. Howe, are of the common compact magnetite from localities in the trap:

Quartz	5·46	4·94
Magnesia and traces of lime	1·27	4·84
Oxygen	24·94	25·19
Metallic iron	68·33	65·03

The magnetite also occurs disseminated where no ore is visible, and may be separated by means of a magnet from the powdered trap of several localities.

Red hematite is found at a number of places associated with agate, quartz, and calcite. It is sometimes presented in the form of small crystalline plates, in a granular quartz matrix and sometimes as crystals, apparently showing its derivation from magnetite. Much of the ore is decidedly magnetic, especially the more highly crystalline specimens.

This range of trap extends from Blomidon to Briar Island, a distance of 120 miles, and contains these ores everywhere in it; but as yet no veins have been found large enough to allow of systematic mining.

TITANIFEROUS IRON ORE.

This is found at St. Mary's Bay, west of Digby, as sand, forming bands of irreguar extent in the beach. The indications are extensive, but no attempts have been made to test their value for working. A sample yielded:

Magnetic ironsand, or iserene	30
Non-magnetic, or ilmenite	56
Silicious sand	14

both varieties containing a large amount of titanium and a little magnesia. This ore is reported from Shelburne, on the Atlantic coast, and from Musquodòboit, near Halifax, that from the latter place being a dark grey micaceous schist, holding crystals of magnetite, with titanium in considerable quantity. The writer has also found an ore of similar appearance, near Sutherland's River, Pictou Co., containing decided traces of titanium.

An attempt has recently been made to work titanic iron ore at Bay St. Paul, on the north shore of the Gulf of St. Lawrence. The ore, containing about 36 per cent. of iron, 44 of titanic acid (and, according to Dr. Penny, no manganese, sulphur, or phosphorus), occurs as a bed about 70 feet thick in a rock of anorthosite of Huronian age.

The dimensions of the furnaces are as follows:

Height	30 feet.
Diameter at hearth	4 "
Diameter at boshes	14 "
Diameter at throat	8 "

Each furnace has three tuyeres, the blast being heated by waste gas taken off by a cupped cone, and applied at a pressure of $1\frac{1}{2}$ lb. The fuel used was exclusively charcoal, 200 or 250 bushels being required for each ton of pig. The daily product of each furnace did not exceed five tons. The pig made was white and of fair quality; but the large amount of fuel used presented a formidable obstacle to profitable working. The following is an analysis of the pig by Mr. Edward Riley:

Carbon	3·966
Silicon	·086
Sulphur	·030
Phosphorus	·253
Chromium	·689
Manganese } Titanium }	traces.
Iron	96·245

The beneficial effects of titanium, formerly dwelt upon, are hardly borne out by practice, and it may, perhaps, be more justly regarded as a foreign ingredient that must be made to pass into the slag, thereby causing a loss of heat.

While in this connection, it may be stated that iron sand is found at various places along the Gulf of St. Lawrence, the Atlantic coast of Nova Scotia, the Bras d'Or Lake, at Amaguadees Pond, and the west coast of Newfoundland, where in many places the iron sand is chiefly composed of magnetic ore.

The ores of Clementsport, near Annapolis, next claim attention. Here a narrow belt of strata of Devonian age, according to Dr. Dawson, three to five miles wide, rises from under the Trias of the Annapolis Valley, and pursues an east and west course for about sixty miles. At one point it is divided by a mass of granite into two nearly equal portions. In the western division are the Clementsport, and in the eastern the Nictaux ores.

At Clementsport there are two beds of ore running nearly east and west, and underlying to the south at angles of 75 to 80 degrees. The highest of these, the Milner bed, varies in thickness from two to four feet. It is specular ore metamorphosed with magnetic properties, and still retaining casts of virelebite, spirifers, and associated mollusks. The ore, which is of fair quality, yields about 33 per cent. of metallic iron. It is mined by open cast, and costs $1.40 per ton for extraction.

The Potter bed is a magnetite (?), and presents the following section where worked :

	Ft.	In.
Ore	3	0
Slate	2	6
Ore	3	6
	9	0

It is compact, and of a dark grey color. The writer has seen no analysis of it, but it is stated to yield 15 per cent more iron than the Milner bed.

BLOOMFIELD BOG ORE.

This is found at several places in the vicinity of the above deposits, and yields 25 per cent. of iron. It occurs in layers, six inches to two feet thick, covered by a few inches of soil. Considerable quantities of it have been extracted at a cost of 40 cts. per ton, for mixture with the other ores.

A blast-furnace was erected here about twenty years ago, and has been running several times since. It is of similar dimensions to those built at Bay St. Paul, but $2\frac{1}{2}$ feet narrower at the boshes. The blast is supplied by a water-wheel through three tuyeres, at a pressure of $1\frac{3}{4}$ to 2 ℔s.

The blowing cylinders are three in number, of cast iron, four feet in diameter, and four feet stroke. The blast is heated by burning the waste gas in an oven with seventeen syphon pipes. Mixtures of all the ores are smelted, yielding an average of 35 per cent of iron. 130 (Winchester) bushels of birch charcoal, costing 4 to 6 cts. per bushel, are required to make one ton of grey pig. There are forty-five charges in twenty-four hours, consisting of from 700 to 800 lbs. ore, 120 lbs. limestone, and 16 bushels of charcoal, yielding daily about five tons. These ores cost at the furnace, including mining and hauling two to four miles, from $1.00 to $1.75. Indications of the eastern extension of these ores are met in the vicinity of Annapolis, and elsewhere in the South Mountain range.

At Nictaux, 37 miles east of Clementsport, a furnace was built to work similar ores, but is now abandoned. The bed which was worked to supply the furnace is a highly fossiliferous peroxide of iron, associated with coarse dark slates, dipping S. 50° E., at an angle of 60°. It has been traced about four miles, and found to vary in thickness from three to four and a half feet.

Dr. Dawson states that the fossils of the red hematite and associated beds are Spirifer arenosus, Strophomena depressa, Strophomena magnifica, Atrypa unguiformis, and species of Avicula, Bellerophon, Favosites and Zaphrentis, Tentaculites, and a coral considered by Mr. Billings identical with the Pleuro-dictyum problematicum, *Goldfuss*. These Professor Hall compares with the fauna of the Oriskany Sandstones, and they seem clearly to prove that the beds of Clements and Nictaux are of lower Devonian age. It may be remarked that Dr. Dawson's conclusions are questioned by Dr. Honeyman, who is inclined to consider these ferriferous strata of much greater age.

The public will await with interest the results of the work of the Canadian Geological Survey, which will, with the aid of their systematic surveys and levels, define more closely the lines of contact of the various systems than any labours of unaided individuals.

Should it eventually prove that iron ore beds of more than one age are present in this district, the extent of ore-bearing ground will be greatly extended both in Nova Scotia and Cape Breton, where the last report of the Geological Survey indicates beds compared with the Devonian of other localities.

The per-centage of iron realized in working was about 50 per cent., but the amount of phosphorus present, and the expense of transport, were against the success of the enterprise. Purer ores are now known in the district, and it is intersected by a railway, so that the proposed resumption of smelting has more chance of succeeding.

*In 1855, Dr. Jackson, State Assayer for Massachusetts, wrote: " One cannot fail to be surprised at the enormous quantities of ore which are already exposed by the numerous openings which have been made. There are several distinct and parallel beds of iron ore which we examined, from four to ten feet in width, extending, certainly, no less than five miles continuously. * * The supply of iron ores at Nictaux is inexhaustible." A short time before, Dr. Hayes described the ores of Nictaux, and spoke of the magnetite on the west side of the river, of the less compact bright red ore of Little River, and of the bog ore of the valley. Mr. Mushet, writing to Mr. C. Archibald, said: "The shell ore is quite a novelty, and the magnetic character of some of the pieces contrasts strongly with the inert state of others to all appearance of similar composition. I have examined it, and find that it is curiously composed of magnetic and non-magnetic laminæ. The assay of the former give $67\frac{3}{4}$ per cent. of iron, and the latter 54 per cent."

The promoters of the Nictaux and Atlantic Railway, now being constructed from Nictaux to Bridgewater, turned their attention, in 1870, to the magnetic ores of the Cleveland Mountain, as far as Lawrencetown, a distance of 6 miles to the west of the river, where the strata are finally cut off by the granite. In the neighbourhood of the river they exposed many beds of ores, ranging in width up to 12 feet. The general course of the metalliferous belt is N. 55° E. Six miles east of the river the transition of the magnitites into hematites takes place. On Foster's farm (late N. Parker), the fossiliferous ore of the character described by Mr. Mushet, is met with, and within 100 yards of it, on the same course east, red hematite makes its first appearance. West from this point, on the Canaan road, fossils are abundant in the magnetite, but they become less and less distinct, until beyond the river all trace of them has disappeared from the magnetites. The hematite beds have been exposed on the farms of David, John and Ingraham Banks, 4 miles east of Canaan, on the Williams River; and they have also been reported at Aylesford, 4 miles further east. One bed is highly fossiliferous, the others are compact and readily cleaved. Meadowvale, where this ore was opened, is only some two miles from the Annapolis Railway.

Bog ore of superior quality is found in the valley at several places between the farm of E. Payson, at Meadowvale; and J. Wheelock's, at Middleton; and on to J. Beales', at Inglesville, a distance of 10 to 12 miles. The ore is of the character called "Pitchy Hydrate," and affords 47 per cent of iron.

* H. S. Poole, Esq., Report Department of Mines, 1877.

It is to be hoped that some of these ores will be found adapted for exportation; and in this event, the proposed railway will afford a convenient outlet to a shipping place. Their character will be seen from the following analyses, by Dr. Waltz, of New York, and Dr. Drown, of Philadelphia:

	Magnetic Black Oxide.		Red Oxide.	
Metallic Iron..................	59·11	53·14	58·05	57.93
Silica........................	11·64	....	....	17·21
Sulphur	·09	....	....	·036
Phosphorus	·17	·172	·193	·16
Alumina.....................	....	....	....	....
Lime........................	....	....	....	....
Magnesia....................	....	....	....	....
Oxide of Manganese..........	...	....	....	....

The ores of this district appear to have been originally red hematites or peroxides, but they have more or less lost part of their oxygen and become magnetic. Specimens can be got showing the gradual change from normal hematites, with cherry-red powder, to magnetic ores, with brown or black streaks. This is probably a local metamorphism, due to the presence of organic matter and the granite dykes which traverse the rocks in the vicinity.

From the country lying to the south of the district above described, and extending to the east as far as Windsor, the writer has received specimens of red hematite, specular and bog ore. As yet, these ores are not known to exist in quantity, but there has been no inducement to search for the beds in situ.

At Goshen, between Windsor and Truro, a vein of ankerite containing limonite has been opened in strata of the Marine Limestone age, and proved to be 40 feet wide. The following analysis of the ore is interesting from the amount of manganese present. In connection with this ingredient, it may be stated that large quantities of manganite and pyrolusite have been mined and exported from this district.

Metallic iron.............................	35·10
Oxides of Manganese......................	24·74*
Alumina.................................	3·68
Lime....................................	·35
Magnesia................................	4·76
Silica	4·81

* Other analyses give ·5 to 1·5 Oxide of Manganese, and larger per centages of iron.

Iron pyrites	·20
Phosphoric acid	·21
Water	11·10

At the mouth of the Shubenacadie river, the lowest visible carboniferous bed is a dark laminated limestone, which, with the overlying sandstones and marls, contains small veins holding limonite and specular ore, with ankerite, barite, calcite, goethite, manganite, and siderite. In the same formation, a few miles to the eastward at Clifton, similar ores are found. At this point they are of more importance, one of the limonite veins being six feet wide.

At Brookfield, ten miles south of Truro, in measures of the same age, and near the contact of older strata, are extensive surface indications of limonite. As yet but little has been done to test the deposits. An engineer of some repute in reporting on the property said: "I consider that the indications of an extensive deposit are greater than even at the Londonderry Mines." This deposit is very favorably situated, being only two miles from the Intercolonial Railway, and about forty-five miles from the Pictou coal field. The ore is of unusually good quality, as will be seen from the analysis of Dr. How, of King's College.

Water	11·36
Silica & Gangue	1·54
Phosphoric acid	trace.
Sulphuric acid	none.
Magnesia	trace.
Peroxide of iron	87·10
	100·00
Metallic iron	60

STEEL COMPANY OF CANADA, LONDONDERRY.

The next ores to be noticed are these limonite deposits, which are hardly equalled for extent, facility of access, and uniformity of quality. At the mines, the Cobequid Hills, marking the division between the watersheds of the Gulf of St. Lawrence and the Basin of Minas, form an immense mass of Upper or Middle Silurian (?) strata, highly metamorphosed, and containing dykes of syenite, etc.

The southern slope of these hills feeds numerous large brooks, which have cut for themselves channels, frequently 300 feet deep, and which afford unusual facilities for tracing the ore, as well as for studying its position. A good idea of its mode of occurrence may be gathered from the section exposed in the brook near the site of the old charcoal furnace.

Here is a series of red and grey shales and sandstones of lower carboniferous age, dipping south at an angle of 60° lying on vertical black and olive slates and quartzites of the Upper Silurian age, striking north 31° east. This line of contact has been traced about twelve miles along the hill sides, or across the property of the company, and affords a key to the position of the ore vein, which is always found in the Silurian strata, at a distance varying from 300 to 500 yards from the lowest met carboniferous bed. Another parallel vein is known one-half mile further north, but has not yet received attention, owing to the ample supply at present developed.

The vein rock consists of a mass of ankerite, varying in width from 30 to 150 feet, and holding in places brecciated masses of quartzite and slate. The ore occurs in minor veins in the ankerite, and is found to be from 5 to 50 feet in width. The chief ore is limonite, which is found in* the botryoidal, stalactitic and compact form, but considerable quantities of micaceous hematite have been met.*

The following are analyses of the two chief ores met:

	Limonite.	Micaceous Hematite.
Peroxide of iron	82.65	96·93
Oxide of Manganese	·25	....
Alumina	·56	·33
Lime	·15	·04
Magnesia	·10	·11
Phosphoric acid	·38	·07
Sulphuric acid	·02	·03
Water, hygroscopic	·31	·03
Water, combined	10·51	·79
Insoluble	4·79	1·26
Metallic iron	57·85	67·85

The following analyses of the Ankerite and Sideroplesite, which form the bed rock of the ores, are from an interesting paper on these deposits read by Mr. H. Louis, late Analyst to the Steel Co. of Canada, before the Nova Scotia Institute of Natural Science, March, 1879:

	Ankerite.	Siderophlestie·
Insoluble Silicious matter	·57	·47
Calcic Carbonate	53·64	·59
Ferrous "	23·29	69·20
Manganous Carbonate	·77	1·37
Magnesic "	21·48	28·73
Ferric oxide	trace.	·08

* For a very full account of this deposit, see Dawson's Acadian Geology.

The latter, which is a variety of siderite, is becoming so abundant in place of the ankerite that it is anticipated that it will prove a valuable ore, when the lower parts of the deposit are reached by the miners.

The ore is won by levels driven to cut it at depths of 200 or 300 feet, and workings adapted to the shape and size of the deposits.

For many years this large body of ore supplied only a small charcoal furnace, from which about 40,000 tons of excellent pig were made, the following analysis of which is by Tookey:

Carbon	3·50
Silica	·84
Sulphur	·02
Phosphorus	·19
Manganese	·44
Iron	94.85

The furnace is similar to that erected at Clementsport, already referred to, and is supplied with cold blast by means of a water-wheel.

The following are the amounts of ore, fuel, and flux used in August, 1873 :—

Ore—Limonite	421·3	
Fuel—Charcoal	32·000.00	bushels (Imperial.)
Flux—Ankerite	68·7	tons.
Pig iron made	221.00	tons, or 7·13 tons daily.

From which the estimated cost of a ton of pig iron would be about $19.00.

Recently the property, embracing 55 square miles of freehold, has been purchased by a number of gentlemen, forming the Steel Company of Canada. Since that date the property has been developed on a scale commensurate with its importance, and numerous levels have exposed large bodies of limonite, affording a supply sufficient for years of steady work.

The following items are from the Reports of the Department of Mines :

A narrow gauge railway, $2\frac{1}{2}$ miles long, has been built from the west mines to the furnace, and a broad guage line, 5 miles long, from the east mines to Debert Station, on the Intercolonial Railway, beside a branch 3 miles long from Londonderry Station to the works.

Two blast-furnaces, 65 feet high, 19 feet in diameter at the boshes, and 5 feet at the hearth, have been built, and are expected to yield 650 tons a week.

Since 1876, 99,366 tons of ore have been smelted, which have yielded about 40,000 tons of pig iron.

The materials smelted in 1877, were:

Iron ore	20,270
Ankerite	1,850
Limestone	6,520
Coke	15,970
Iron made	9,863

The blast has a pressure of 2-4 lbs. heated in three Cowper Siemens' stoves to from 800°–1100° Fahr.

The blowing engine has the steam cylinder above the blowing cylinder, which has a stroke of 5 feet, and a diameter of 6 feet.

Water is brought in a flume 3460 feet to the blast furnace, and 4060 feet to the rolling mill.

There have been built six single puddling furnaces and one double, two more double furnaces are in process of construction; and there is one heating furnace—in all having a capacity of 25 tons of finished iron per day.

There are two trains of rolls, one 9 inch and one 16 inch trains; two steam hammers, one 20 cwt., and one 50 cwt.

The bar iron made, according to Riehle Bros. tests, is "ductile and fine grained;" Tensile strength 60,000 lbs. per square inch, and elongation 33 per cent. The "Best Best" iron has been used to replace Lowmoor and Swedish iron. The following analyses by Mr. Louis shew the high character of the pig and bar iron:

	No. 1 Pig Iron.	Siemans' Best Bar Iron
Silicon	3·621....(part slag)	·280
Graphitic Carbon	3·730	
Combined Carbon	·390	·096
Sulphur	·002	trace.
Phosphorus	·198	·035
Manganese	1·126	·041
Iron	90·933	99·548
	100·000	100·800

There have been erected at the works 42 bee-hive coke ovens, having each a capacity of 6 tons of coal.

Several furnaces have been built for the Siemans' direct process, and are understood to have given satisfactory results.

The fuel used is coke from the Main Seam, Pictou Co., already referred to, and coal from the Intercolonial Mine, coked at the works. A certain per-centage of raw coal is also used, and has been found to work satisfactorily.

The quality of the pig and bar iron, etc., made at these works by various processes, is of the very best, and adapted for every work requiring those qualities which, seldom attainable except at ruinous prices and by means of expensive mixtures, are here presented ready for the smelter. The report of the Canadian Gun Works, at Montreal, on the quality of the Londonderry bar iron used in the process of converting the old cast iron 62 pounders, shows that its quality is superior to that of the best English and American iron.

The Londonderry ores are known, from surface indications, to extend over twenty-five miles to the west of the lands controlled by this company, but no attempt has been made to prove their extent.

In the natural sections of the carboniferous measures exposed at the Joggins, are numerous balls and irregular bands of ironstone, not, however, yet considered of economic importance.

At various points in the carboniferous district of this County, are found deposits of bog ore, but their extent and quality are unknown, Other localities that have yielded specimens of iron ore are, Clark's Point, Parrsboro, Joggins, Cape Sharp, Fullerton's Lake, etc.

PICTOU COUNTY.—IRON ORES.

The iron ores of this district are more varied and of greater extent than elsewhere in the Province, and, from their relation to fuel, flux, and shipping, are destined to play an important part in its future development.

Although the existence of iron ores on the East River of Pictou was known for many years, it was not until 1872 that any systematic attempts were made to test their extent. As early as 1828, or shortly after the General Mining Association of London opened their Pictou collieries, a blast furnace was erected at the colliery, and a small quantity of red hematite and limonite smelted; but the expenses of hauling the ore twelve miles, soon put an end to the work. Nothing was then done until, in 1872-3, extensive explorations were carried on under the supervision of Dr. Dawson, and continued for several years from that date by the writer.

Taking the ores in descending geological order, the first to be noticed are the bog ores. These are scattered over many parts of the county, notably on the West Branch and the head waters of River John. Several small deposits have been found near French River, of which an analysis, by the writer, is given below. They also occur north of New Glasgow, and are apparently derived from the conglomerate already referred to, as limiting the coal field.

We have next to notice the Clay Ironstone ores of the Pictou coal field. They form irregular beds from 5 to 40 in. thick, and are found everywhere in the coal measures, in some cases forming part of the seams. But little attention has yet been paid to them. From the writer's analysis given below it will be seen that they are of good quality, and is it considered that they will prove an important addition to the older ores.

At French River, in the Marine Limestone formation (?), are numerous beds of Clay Ironstone Carbonates, and Hydrated Peroxides, in beds from 6 in. to 4 ft. in thickness. The discovery is a recent one and little is yet known about the deposits. The following analysis is by the writer

	Bog ore French River	Clay Ironstone Pictou Coal Field.	Black Band Pictou Coal Field.	Clay Ironstone French River.
Moisture	5·500	2·132	·732	......
Water of comp :...	6·100	....	....	......
Sulphur	·208	·612	·214	·022
Phosphoric Acid....	·384	trace	·586	trace
Manganese.......	5.886	....	4·450	......
Lime	trace	trace	3.780	......
Magnesia........	trace	1·655	·783	trace
Alumina	3·106	16·962	3·180	2·718
Silica............	12·325	·780	16·546	58·800
Carbonic acid.....	....	....	27·589	3·370
Iron protoxide	....	45·361	36·000	......
Iron peroxide....	66·510	....	....	35.942
	100·019	67·502	100·000	99·852
Metallic iron......	46·557	35·000	28·000	25.16

Passing to the westward, a large deposit of spathic ore is found at Sutherland's Brook, held by the Pictou Coal and Iron Co. The containing strata were formerly considered of Millstone grit age; but, from the proximity of gypsum and limestone, they would seem rather to belong to the Marine Limestone formation. As far as can be judged from a rough survey, this ore is found at a horizon 800 feet lower than the Ironstone of French River.

The bed dips south at an angle of 60 degrees, and varies in thickness from 6 to 10½ feet, and has above and below a small bed of the same, 6 to 10 inches thick. The ore is a sparry carbonate of iron, holding peroxide in places, with a variable proportion of manganese, and very little sulphur and phosphorus. Superficially it is rusted, but where unweathered, of a pearly grey colour. From surface indications, it appears probable that this ore extends over a considerable district, and the writer is inclined to consider it characteristic of a horizon low down in the Marine Limestone.*

Analyses of Spathic Ore from Sutherland's Brook.

	I. Dr. S. Hunt,	II. T. E. Thorpe.
Sesquioxide of iron	20·52	......
Carbonate of iron	57·40	88·59
Carbonate of manganese	8·29	2·85
Carbonate of lime	4·02	1·53
Carbonate of magnesia	5·66	3·48
Silica	2.38	2·70
Moisture	1·43	55
Sulphur	None	......
Phosphorus	None	......
Iron	42·07	42·76

From Springville for several miles up the East River, the line of contact of the Marine Limestone and Silurian follows closely the course of the river. At several points along this line a very fine deposit of Limonite has been proved. On the property of the Halifax Co., some years ago, the writer proved it to have a thickness of 21 feet 6 inches, and recent researches have proved it to be 15 feet thick on the Saddler area of the Pictou Coal and Iron Co., and an equal development at other points.

The ore is compact, concretionary, and fibrous, with considerable quantities of gravel ore. At two points the ore has been proved to rest on the Silurian clay slates, and has Limestone on the hanging wall, usually with a gore of red clay, frequently holding concretions of Manganite and Pyrolusite intervening. These ores are very pure, and appear to be much more free from phosphorus than the Londonderry limonite, the average of five analyses of the East River ore giving ·118 phosphoric acid, or ·083 phosphorus, in 100 parts of iron.

* See paper on the "The Limonite and Limestones of Pictou Co.," by E. Gilpin, Transactions N. S. I. N. S., 1878-79.

These ores in places hold notable quantities of Manganese, and resemble closely the Spanish Limonites imported into England. The following analyses of large averages by the writer will show the great purity of these ores, and their Manganese contents.

Analyses of East River Limonites.

Water	7·702	12·530
Iron peroxide	87·925	{ 48.223
Alumina	trace	
Silica	3·000	25·130
Manganese binoxide	trace	14·410
Lime	....	·015
Magnesia	·500	traces.
Sulphur	trace	·480
Phosphorus	trace	·020
	97·127	100·908
Metallic iron	65·54	33·826

The belt holding ore is 600 yards wide at several places, as shown by surface indications, and it appears probable that there is a large amount of it in the valley.

The Limonite may have been derived, like the Limonite of Cumberland district and other localities in Pennsylvania, as a residual precipitate from the disseminated iron sand grains of the Upper Silurian strata as well as a deposit from the gradual dissolution of the Marine Limestones. In view of this, it may be stated that in this district the rocks of both ages contain considerable quantities of iron as carbonate and peroxide, and that the erosion has been on an enormous scale. This has been fully treated of by the writer, in a paper read Feb., 1879, Institute of Natural Science, Halifax.

It may be mentioned here that some of the East River limestones may be found valuable iron ores. An analysis of a bed 12 feet thick near Springville giving the writer the following results:

Moisture	·400
Lime carbonate	55·280
Magnesia. "	10·150
Iron "	24·110
Manganese	1·835
Alumina	4·300
Sulphur	·168
Phosphorus	none
Residue	5·000
	101·243

The district extending from Sunny Brae, nearly to the Spathic ore on Sutherland's Brook, is occupied by grey and brownish quartzites, olive and grey slates with calcareous bands, usually coarse and unevenly bedded, and containing the fossils of the Arisaig group, a series considered equivalent to the Lower Helderberg of American geologists, and, perhaps, in its specific forms more related to the English Ludlow. The following are among the more common fossils of this district: Favosites, Zaphrentis, Chonetes tenuistriata, Spirifer rugæcosta, Strophomena profunda, Rhynchonella spirata, Atrypa reticularis, Athyris didyma, Megambonia striata, trilobata, Orthoceras sev. sp., Cornulites, Dalmania Logani, etc.

The chief ore of this formation is a bedded Red Hematite found in four principal deposits. The most northerly of these is known as the McKenzie red hematite. It appears from surface indications to be of large size, but no work has yet been done to test it.

The next bed, known as the Webster ore, has been carefully trenched and tested at several points, and extends about 3 miles. Its thickness varies from 15 to 30 feet, its dip being generally north at angles varying from 25° to 60.°

At two points it presents the following sections:

	Ft.	In.		Ft.	In.
Ore	4	4	Ore (in four layers)	5	0
Smooth parting	0	0	Smooth parting	0	0
Ore	3	0	Ore	2	6
Slate	2	11	Smooth parting	0	0
Ore	3	3	Ore	3	0
	13	6	Slaty ore	3	10
			Ore	6	0
			Total	20	4

This ore follows the crest of a hill, cut transversely by the valley of Sutherland's River, and admits of adit drainage to a depth of 300 feet. The ore is compact, non-fossiliferous, and brick-red when weathered.

The third exposure is known as the Blanchard great bed. No attempts have yet been made to trace it beyond the natural exposures which extend about half a mile. It varies in width from 30 to 100 feet, measured across a dip nearly vertical. It is also situated on elevated ground, and would yield a large amount of ore.

At a geological horizon about 700 feet higher than the last-mentioned bed is a conformable range of Red Hematites forming the fourth series. This ore appears to form a synclinal trough. On the west side the ore is 12 feet thick; at the apex there appear the outcrops of two other beds eight and three feet in thickness, the larger possibly representing the great bed at Blanchard. On the east of the synclinal, only one bed has been opened, varying in width from three to five feet. Underlying this bed, and on the line where the great bed would show its eastern outcrop, are large boulders, precisely similar in appearance to the ore on its western outcrop, and it is expected that it will shortly be found here.

It is considered by some geologists that the large single beds were originally one, and owe their present disjointed condition to faults and erosion; no detailed survey, however, has been made to prove the correctness of this opinion, and at present it can only be said that they are apparently contained in a limited vertical range of strata. The outcrops of other Red Hematites have been detected, but no work has yet been done to allow of details.

These Red hematites are all of the same class, being of a red color, with earthy to steely lustre, compact or laminated, sometimes oolitic, owing to the peroxide forming minute concretions around grains of sand. In places these ores contain fossils, but the larger proportion are quite free from them. They are excellently adapted for mining, being on high ground, with good roof, and requiring little or no dead work.

Similar ores, called fossil Red Hematites, are found in Pennsylvania, in strata of the Clinton age, and extensively worked near Tyrone, for mixture with rich hematites and Magnetites. The following analysis will show its relation to the Pictou ores, of which analyses are given further on.

Sesquoxide of iron	38·48
Peroxide of iron	4·37
Silica	37·99
Alumina	9·56
Lime	1·08
Alkalies	2·89
Phosphoric acid	1·48
Sulphur	trace
Volatile	4·50
Metallic iron	30·34

Passing to the west side of the East River, the Carboniferous is found resting on a broad belt of black and olive slate, with bands of quartzite, dipping almost vertically to the south. In these measures considered by Dr. Dawson the equivalents of those holding the Londonderry ores, is a large vein of specular ore. The exact relation of these measures to those holding the Red Hematites is not easily ascertained.

as no fossils have yet been found in them, but they appear to occupy a lower position.

The vein shows ore varying in width from 5 to 20 feet; in places there are intercalated masses of quartzite and ankerite. The Pictou Coal and Iron Company own over two miles of this vein, in addition to large and well selected areas on the Limonite, and the Webster and other Red Hematites on the east side of the river.

At two points, a vein of a mixture of specular and magnetic ore, one to two feet thick, has been met, but no work has been done to test its value. The main vein is cut by several ravines, and for some distance runs close to the brow of a hill 200 feet high, which would be found advantageous in mining.

About two and a half miles to the westward, and nearly on the strike of the specular ore, a large body of reddish quartzite is found in similar black slates, and holds several veins of Limonite from one to three feet in thickness. The bed rock has been traced some distance, and is capable of yielding a considerable quantity of ore above water level. The ore is compact, of a chocolate colour, with small cavities lined with crystals and plates of the same mineral.

Near Glengarry, specular ore is again met in small veins, in a yellowish gray quartzite, but no work has yet been done to test its extent.

At numerous other points in the county, rocks of Silurian and Carboniferous age, and some of the traps, contain crystals and veinlets of specular and magnetic ore, as traces of metamorphic action, as well as indications of permanent deposits, but little attention has been paid to them, beyond the district described.

The following analyses, by the writer and others, will show the very high character of the ores just described:

	Specular.		Limonite.		Red Hematite.	
	I.	II.	I.	II.	I.	II.
Oxides of Iron..................	92·01	97·52	93·09	81·19	70·00	65·26
" Magnesia............	2·16	....	1·10	·20	....	trace
Alumina......................	·21	....	....	....	....	5·59
Carbonate of Lime.............	1·27	....	·01	·63	3·03	1·88
" Magnesia..........	·43	....	....	....	....	1·05
Phosphoric Acid......	·08	....	....	·15	·20	....
Sulphur.......................	·16	·06	·04	trace	....	....
Silica.........................	3·68	3·20	4·80	4·26	25·83	25·68
Metallic iron..................	64·41	68·33	65·20	56·83	45·47	43·4

On the St. Mary River, are reported large beds of limonite. At Arisaig, in Upper Silurian strata, a bed of red hematite, three feet thick, has been found. From specimens that the writer has seen, it appears similar in character to the bedded hematites just described, but less silicious. This bed is found at the eastern end of the Lower Helderberg strata just referred to, and in the long range intervening new discoveries may be confidently anticipated.

A large amount of money has been expended in testing the iron ores of Pictou County, and it is to be hoped that, at no distant date, smelting operations will be started. In this county, iron, coal, and limestone are all within a few miles of each other; and there is a ready outlet by rail and water. Certainly, at no other point in the Dominion are the natural facilities greater for such operations; and every visitor to the iron beds is astonished at their extent and value.

There are other ores in the district, specimens of which occur in the drift; but the beds themselves are not yet discovered, so that the field for the iron smelter appears unlimited.

CAPE BRETON.

Our knowledge of the iron ore of this part of the Province, is limited, no work having been done beyond a few trenches across the outcrops of what appear to be promising deposits.

At Loran, near Louisburg, boulders of a compact Red Hematite of excellent quality, have been found, but the writer is not aware of any attempts to prove the ore in situ. Tha following analysis of it is by G. F. Downing, of Workington:

Peroxide of iron	90·14
Lime and Magnesia	4·20
Sulphur	·10
Phosphoric acid	·11
Silica	5·45

This ore resembles some of the Cumberland (England) Red Hematites in appearance and quality.

At the summit of the Lower Carboniferous, as exposed near Sydney, is a thick bed of red marl, with thick nodules of limestone. Near the top of this bed is a hard grey sandstone, containing a variable amount of peroxide of iron, in places equal to 30 per cent. of metallic iron. Attempts to work this ore proved unsuccessful, owing to its irregular quality and distribution.

At Big Pond, East Bay, Bras d'Or Lake, near the contact of Lower Carboniferous Conglomerates and Laurentain measures a deposit of ochreous red hematite, considered to be of large extent, has been tested. The ore, as will be seen from the analysis given further on, is of excellent quality, and should find a ready market as a first-class Bessemer ore.

Near the crossing of the French Vale and Bourinot roads, about 17 miles from Sydney, Hon. Mr. Moseley has tested an important discovery of red hematite in the George River, (Laurentian) limestones. The bed runs north-east, and varies in thickness from five to nine feet, being included between two beds of white and light blue crystaline limestone. The ore is said to have been traced for a considerable distance by pits and exposures. From the analysis given further on, this ore is also a very valuable one, and should find a ready market at Philadelphia and New York.

Hon. Mr. Moseley subsequently discovered the ore on widow Campbell's land, two and a half miles distant, with similar surroundings. This discovery is important, as it offers a hope that similar valuable beds may be found in other exposures of these limestones.

Red hematite is frequently found among the Lower Silurian slates and limestones of St. Andrew's channel, and these may prove workable at some points, as for instance, near McSween's Brook.

Traces of magnetic iron ore and hematite are widely distributed among the marbles of George's River and the limestones of Boularderie.

At Whyhogomah, on the Bras d'Or Lake, on the property of the Inverness Coal and Iron Company, nine deposits have been exposed and proved to form beds in measures of Laurentian age. They were traced some hundreds of yards, when further explorations were stopped by the heavy covering of soil. The ore appears to be a mixture of red hematite and magnetite in varying proportions.

From the analysis by the late Dr. How, and Prof. Hayes, the ore appears to be very free from all impurity, except silica, the proportions of sulphur and phosphorus being small.

A great point in favor of these deposits, and what are supposed to be their continuation in the district, is the presence of deep water within a few hundred yards of the ore, which would allow vessels of large burden to load for distant markets; while it can be carried in scows or barges to any part of the Bras d'Or Lake.

Analyses of Cape Breton Iron Ores.

COMPOSITION.	WHYHOGOMAH.		FRENCH VALE.‡	BIG POND.*
	I.*	II †		
Iron Peroxide....................	68·94	....	85·037	88·21
Oxygen...........................	....	23·30	....	....
Silicious Matter...................	24·78	10·80	5·130	9·04
Water.............................	1·30	....	....	1·53
Alumina..........................	2·72	1·40	....	....
Lime..............................	1·18	1·85	....	....
Magnesia.........................	1·08	1·64	....	1·22
Sulphur...........................	traces	·11	·075	trace
Phosphoric Acid	none	none	·032	trace
Metallic Iron.....................	48·25	60·90	59·526	61·39

Mr. Fletcher, in the Geo. Sur. Rep. 1876-77, writes that the universal occurrence of calcspar and hematite among the Laurentian, Silurian, and Carboniferous measures of Cape Breton County is remarkable. To the latter all the red rocks owe their color, and in places it separates into veins and strings. Near McDougal's Point, Big Pond, a limited deposit of excellent quality was seen at the junction of Carboniferous conglomerate with Syenite; at McNeil's mill, on the Glengarry road, similar traces have been met; and large boulders occur at Loch Lomond post office. It is also present in the limestone of Boularderie, most of the Lower Silurian rocks, and many of the pre-Silurian felsites, in many cases, however, too much disseminated to be of economic value.

Spathic iron ore occurs with the Lower Carboniferous marine limestones of Island Point, Boularderie, in a bed 2 to 3 feet thick, yielding 32·58 per cent. of metallic iron. In this connection, reference may be made to the spathic ores of Pictou County.

Bog Iron ore is found in a bed 2 feet thick, at J. McSween's, Fox Brook, Boisdale, and in a marsh near the Bourinot road, and at several points on Indian Brook. A deposit of excellent quality has been observed near Schooner Pond.

Iron ores are reported from many other localities in Cape Breton, but as yet little work has been done in the way of testing their extent and quality.

In the following table are the names of places affording iron ore, of which there is not much known :

* Dr. How.   † Prof. Hayes.   ‡ Dr. Harrington.

Locality.	Geological Age.	Ore.	Metallic per-cent-age.	Remarks.
Newton Mills, Stewiacke,	Lower Carboniferous	Limonite...........	......	
Lochaber.......	Upper Silurian?....	Specular Spathic	......	In veins and as matrix of copper ores.
W't Branch Lake	Upper Silurian......	Limonite........	·56	Small Veins.
New Glasgow...	Upper Coal Measures	Bog Ore. Clay Ironstone.	30·55	Quantity small.
Green Hill......	do. do.	Limonite	......	Vein said to be 6 in. thick.
Merigomish.....	Lower Carboniferous	Hematite.........	......	As pebbles in Conglomerate resting on Silurian Strata.
Antigonish......	....	Bog Ore........	45·00	
Guysboro.......	Lower Carboniferous	Specular	60·00	
Shelburne River.	....	Bog Ore.........	......	
Port La Tour...	....	do.	......	
Lunenburg Co...	....	do.	......	
Walton.........	Lower Carboniferous	Limonite.........	......	Reported large quant'y
Grand Anse....	....	Hematite........	......	
Cape St. Lawr'ce	....	Magnetite......	......	
Mabou..........	Coal Measures......	Clay Ironstone..	42·00	Quantity small.
Loch Lomond...	Devonian?..........	Manganiferous Limonite	......	
Sydney.........	Lower Carboniferous	Clay Ironstone...	......	
Barrasois........	Coal Measures......	do. ...	27.89	Quantity small.
Schooner Pond..	do.	Bog Ore. Clay Ironstone.	35·00 25·84	do.
Gabarus.........	....	Hematite.......	......	Quantity unknown.
Grand River....	Devonian...........	"	......	Quantity small.
Lake Ainslie....	....	Limonite........	......	Quantity said to be large.

As the labours of the Canadian Geological Survey have been confined as yet to a small portion of the Province, it would be premature to venture to point out localities likely to contain iron ore beyond those described by Dr. Honeyman and Principal Dawson. The discoveries by Hon. Mr. Mosely, referred to above, are among the most important, for they lead to a hope that the Laurentian, or according to the proposed grouping of the survey, the Huronian strata of Nova Scotia, may be found specially worthy of the attention of the miner. The most important of the Canadian iron ores are found in strata of this age, and the catalogue of Canadian Minerals sent to the Philadelphia Exhibition, contains notices of many such deposits.

In the various divisions of the Silurian strata, stretching from Canso to Yarmouth, beds and veins of iron ore occur, and the point or vicinity of contact of these measures with the carboniferous has frequently shown evidence of valuable deposits. The gold-producing rocks of the Atlantic coast have, so far, I believe, not yielded deposits of ore considered of workable size.

Deposits of bog ore are found scattered in all parts of the Province; few of the beds have been tested, but should any demand arise, a very considerable quantity could be obtained for mixtures with other ores.

When the lack of interest, the want of information, and the thinly settled state of the Province are considered, it must be admitted that the discoveries made promise well for the future. As the country gets more settled, fresh discoveries may be anticipated, for nearly all the ores mentioned above were disclosed by the plough or natural exposures, and as the greater part of the Province likely to contain ores is wooded, there will probably be no deficiency of the raw material.

It may be anticipated that the effect of the protection imposed by the Dominion, on the manufacture of iron, will shortly have the effect of inducing the opening and working of some of the above described deposits.

When it is considered that the value of the imports of iron, raw, partly and completely manufactured, was, during the fiscal year, 1877, $10,400,000; 1878, $9,215,000; and 1879, $7,916,846; it will be seen that an ample field is open for our iron workers.

When once such operations are commenced, it will be found that many of our ores offer facilities for the manufacture of high grades of iron and steel which can be exported. There can be no doubt that the increasing advantages steamers offer for freighting will cause our shipbuilders to consider if they cannot build iron vessels here also. In no long lapse of time, unless they do so, the Province must gradually lose its present profitable business of building and sailing vessels.

In this connection, the important fact must not be forgotten, that in Nova Scotia alone, of all the Provinces of the Dominion, the ores, fuels and fluxes occur close together, and therefore it is from this Province that Canada must draw its future supplies of iron.

THE COPPER ORES OF NOVA SCOTIA.

Although for many years the presence of various ores of copper was known in this Province, it is but recently that discoveries of economic value have been made.

In the early French expeditions to Canada and Acadie (now Nova Scotia) were men similar to those styled by Sir Humphrey Gilbert "rare refiners of mines;" and their reports on the supposed mineral wealth of Nova Scotia and Cape Breton excited much interest in Paris, and formed one of the reasons that France struggled so strongly to retain her supremacy in British America.

Lescharbot, writing in 1609, speaks of the native copper of the Bay of Fundy as being "very pure in the stone," and adds, "many goldsmiths have seen it in France, which do say that under the copper mine there might be a golden mine, which is very probable."

The stone he alludes to is the trap associated with the Triassic sandstones of the Bay of Fundy; copper is found scattered through it in small grains and lumps, but has not yet been found in workable quantity. Much money has been spent at various times in testing these indications. As is usually the case with copper ores, many deposits, at first very promising, have proved valueless; but some have been found under workable conditions.

In this Province, the ores occur in rocks of every geological age met in descending order, from the Triassic downward.

The trap of the Bay of Fundy has, as already noticed, from the earliest days of our history, yielded grains and lumps of metallic copper, sometimes weighing fifty pounds. Attempts were made, some years ago, to mine it near Margaretsville, on the shore of Annapolis County. The copper occurred, associated with zeolites and other infiltrates, but it proved to be too irregularly scattered in the matrix to permit systematic mining. It is found at many other places, among which may be mentioned Cape d'Or, Spencer's Island, Five Islands, Briar Island, etc.

The trap of this locality is considered to differ widely in age from that associated with the Huronian copper-bearing strata of Lake Superior, which has yielded the metal from pre-historic times. But, when it is found in the Bay of Fundy trap, at so many localities, there will always be a strong inducement to test the more promising exposures; and it may be found in places to be scattered in the trap, in fine grains, in quantity sufficient to allow of its being profitably extracted.

It may be mentioned, in this connection, that I have observed metallic copper in dendritic forms in the copper ores of Antigonish County, and Mr. Barnes reported finding it near Cheticamp, Cape Breton.

The upper and lower coal measures of Pictou, Cumberland and other counties, frequently show outcrops of nests and layers of the vitreous sulphuret and green carbonate of this metal, associated with jet-like coaly matter. These deposits are believed to have originally consisted of accumulations of vegetable matter, in the swamps and estuaries of that age, and afterwards when the strata became solidified, that the ores of copper were deposited from their aqueous solutions, through the not yet clearly understood medium of the carbonaceous matter they have now partly or completely replaced.

Such deposits have been observed and tested at many points in the Province, among which I may mention the East River of Pictou, near Hopewell, and below Springville, West River, near Durham.

The following is Dr. Dawson's analysis of a sample of these ores, from Carribou, near Pictou:

Copper	40·00
Iron	11·06
Cobalt	2·10
Manganese	·50
Sulphur	25·42
Lime	·92
Carbonic acid, Silica, etc.	20·00
	100·00

Other localities are Salmon River, near Truro; Athole, Stewiacke, etc. An interesting deposit, belonging to this class, is found on French River, above Tatamagouche. Here, in the upper coal measures, are several beds of argillaceous sandstone, and conglomerates, holding nodules and seams of vitreous copper and green carbonate, associated with so-called lignite.

The ore is rich, holding up to 74 per cent. of metallic copper, and should the deposits prove persistent, might be profitably mined for treatment by a wet process. Several attempts have been made to work these deposits, hitherto, without success; another trial, I understand, is to be made during this year; it is to be hoped with better results.

I give the following description of the locality from the Report of the Dept. of Mines, 1877:

"Mr. Patterson, in 1857, got a thirty years' lease of this locality, but then did no more than extract a sample of both qualities to send to England. In return he was advised that the nodular ore was the most valuable and would command a ready sale; but he let the property lie idle till 1866, when some six men were constantly employed during the summer, chiefly in working out the north-west side of the river at a spot where the bank is steep and about 60 feet high. Shallow drifts and shafts were driven and sunk to prove the deposit, but of the results I have no information. Nor that further work was done until 1876-77, when six months work of twelve men produced, according to the statement of Mr. Prendergast, the manager, some 36 casks of ore, each averaging about 900 lbs. Subsequent work for two months yielded 6 more casks, averaging 800 lbs. each, or a total of 18½ tons, valued at New York at $120 per ton. "The excavations made, extended along the bank about 400 feet, and in laid over 200 feet, in length they measured nearly 2000 feet.

"Across the river some work was also done, but as in 1866, it did not prove so remunerative, only one bed, and that small, containing noudules.

"On the west side the grey sandstone beds near the top of the bank, carry the nodules disseminated through them to a depth of about 4 feet, the principal deposit being in a dark grey bed from 8 to 10 inches thick. Owing to the action of subærial agents, the bed has a greenish caste, and the nodules are coated with carbonate. In composition both the mono and disulphide occur; Mr. Louis, the analyst at Londonderry, was the first to detect the presence of covelline.* The nodules are on an average small, not larger than cherries, though some have been found weighing one and a half pounds. When I visited this locality the drifts had so fallen in that it was impossible to estimate the apparent extent of the deposit, but from what was to be seen, it appeared not improbable that the nodules were not equally disseminated throughout the bed in which they are found, but are collected together, as it were, at eddies or banks in the sandstone deposit. Below the grey beds, come beds of a reddish color, and below them, close to the river's edge, other grey beds in which are the remains of plants, the tissue of which has become filled with copper pyrites.

"At Waugh's River, and at other places in the neighbourhood, copper ore thus associated has been found. It has been worked on Waugh's River about three-quarters of a mile from New Annan, and in 1877, some eight barrels of ore were collected, weighing about three tons and valued at $30 per ton."

Very similar ores occur in millstone grit, in Westmoreland County, N. B., and samples are reported by the Provincial Assayist to yield 15 per cent. of silver.

In Kings County, at East Dalhousie, a lode of quartz, associated with granite in pre-carboniferous measures, has been sunk on during the past year to a depth of about 95 feet. The ores are vitreous and gray, sulphurets; and blue and green carbonates. Assays show the presence of silver up to 25 oz. per ton of 2000 ℔s. At many points through the district strong indications of copper ore are found, and should the present prospecting show workable deposits, they would probably also receive attention.

Mr. Poole, in his report on the Western Gold Fields, in 1862, mentions finding copper pyrites in slates at Blandford Cove, Lunenburg Co.,

---

* Covelline is a sulphide of copper formed by removal of part of the copper in the vitreous ore; he mineral in question held 64·11 per cent. of copper.

Hillsboro Brook, Westfield Brook, Geyser's Hill, Jebogue Point. It is also a common mineral in the gold-bearing lodes of the Province.

The head waters of the East River of Pictou have yielded specimens of copper pyrites, with spathose iron gangue, but no attempts have been made to search for their source.

In the vicinity of the Garden of Eden, several localities have been observed, holding veins of spar, up to several feet in thickness, with crystals of copper pyrites. The only deposits which have been tested to any extent are those of Antigonish County, where large sums of money have been spent, and a considerable tract of county proved to be cupriferous. At Lochaber, on the property controlled by Messrs. McBean, Fraser, and others, of New Glasgow, the explorations so far as carried show a series of veins, cutting at oblique angles black and red shales and quartzites, and thrown for a short distance 30° out of an east-and-west course by a dyke, apparently a diorite containing talc and serpentine.

The first vein met going east is about 2 feet wide. I have no details of its contents. The second vein, 80 feet distant, has been proved to a depth of 85 feet; it varies in width from 5 feet 6 inches to 6 feet 3 inches, and holds about 20 per cent. of copper pyrites, evenly distributed in talcose slate, greenstone, and quartz, and micaceous iron ore. The third vein, 216 feet distant, is from 1 foot 6 inches to 2 feet wide, and holds copper pyrites, with erubescite in bands, with quartz and talcose greenstone. The fourth vein, 130 feet distant, is about 5 feet wide, and carries about 10 per cent. of rich ore with much quartz. The fifth and sixth veins are respectively 50 and 150 feet further east; they are about each 3 feet wide. The leads also contain large per-centages of ore, but have not yet been examined. In these last, the micaceous ore has been, to some extent, replaced by carbonate of iron, which is the chief gangue of the Polson's Lake ore. The sixth vein is gradually returning to its east-and-west course; and, at a further distance of 300 yards, it has been opened again, and proved to be 4 feet 6 inches wide; and, nearly half a mile to the east, on the strike of the vein, two small veins have been found, holding very good ore, and large boulders proving the passage of the larger veins.

The quality of the Lochaber ore is unusually good; the chief variety met is copper pyrites, with a small admixture of carbonate of copper and erubescite. The gangue at Lochaber is chiefly micaceous iron ore,' with a little spathic ore; at Polson's Lake, exclusively the latter.

An average of the large veins gave, on analysis, by Dr. How, of Windsor:

Metallic copper	19·21
Metallic iron	25·31
Sulphur	22·65
Carbonate of lime	5·15
Oxygen	4·07
Gangue	23·01
	99·40

An analysis of the pyrites from the second vein gave the writer: *

Copper	29·00
Iron	29·70
Sulphur	31·50
Silica	3·40
Moisture	·20
Carbonate of iron	6·20
	100·00

A sample from the third vein gave, at Swansea, 31·25 of metallic copper.

The course of the cupriferous band has been traced, by surface-indications, from this point, about four miles, to Polson's Lake where, during the past summer, a very fine vein of spathic ore, holding copper pyrites, and a little iron pyrites, was traced for several hundred feet through dark blue and olive slates. Its width varied from 6 to 11 feet; and its course was about N. 70° W. (astr.). Dr. Dawson gives the average of copper in this ore at 10·8 per cent. The explorations were carried on by the parties already mentioned, and by Mr. W. Ross, of Pictou.

The following notes are by Dr. Harrington (G. S. R. 1876-77, p. 476). The first sample, taken at a considerable depth from the surface, where the vein was 11 feet thick, yielded 11·7 of copper, but no silver. The second sample was from the surface, and consisted of copper pyrites, pale iron pyrites, hydrated peroxide of iron, and rock matter; it yielded 5·67 per cent of copper, and, I believe, no silver.

On the Salmon River, the Primrose property shows a small vein, which was tested to some extent a few years ago, and contains very rich copper ore. From analyses made by Dr. Hayes, State Analyst, Boston,

* Notes on Discoveries of Copper Ore in Nova Scotia, by E. Gilpin, Quarterly Journal Geological Society of London, Nov., 1877.

U. S., the ore contained from 37 to 39 per cent. of copper, and was composed of copper pyrites and erubescite.

The age of the strata holding these deposits is not yet definitely known, as no systematic geological survey has been made of this part of the Province. The sandstones, shales, limestones, and bedded diorites, etc., very strongly resemble the Eastern Townships copper-bearing rocks.

In Cape Breton, a large number of places are noted in the reports of Mr. Fletcher, of the Geological Survey, as holding copper ores, as traces and deposits possibly of workable extent. Thus he mentions the metal as occurring in traces as copper pyrites in the crystalline rocks of Benacadie, the White Granite Hills; in quartz veins in the Lower Silurian felsites of Gillis' Brook, as green carbonate; in Lower Carboniferous Conglomerates, Spruce Brook, Bras d'Or. In his report 1876-77, he says: "Mention has already been made of a number of places shewing traces of copper glance, oxydised to carbonate, impregnating a conglomerate often at its contact with an overlying bed of limestone, as at Irish Cove, East Bay, Washaback, Middle and North Rivers."

Three assays of samples from the Washaback Conglomerate, near Crow Point, are said to have yielded Dr. Hayes:

1. 5 dwts. of gold per ton.
2. 3-10 of copper, and 19 dwts. 4 grs. of gold per ton.
3. 16 dwts. 8 grs of gold, and 6 dwts. 12 grs. of silver per ton.

Although, in some cases, these deposits may be the remains of plants replaced by metallic ores, as pointed out by Prof. Hynd, in a report on the district, the mineral often forms the matrix of the conglomerate.

Yellow copper pyrites occurs on the farm of Angus McDonald, on the French Road, near Garbarus, as nodules and layers in a compact felsite, occupying a considerable tract of country.

Copper pyrites occurs at Eagle Head, in Gabarus Bay, in a belt of laminated quartz, some 25 feet thick, intermixed with soft feldspathic rock. The quartz layers are of various thicknesses, and carry the ore in irregular quantities. Associated with the band, is a whitish green soapstone with arsenical pyrites, bismuth glance, iron pyrites, molybdenite, and traces of gold. The copper is also met in a light coloured felsite, containing vugs lined with crystals of quartz, and appears to be generally distributed through the neighboring felsites. Shafts have been sunk at the Eagle Head and French Road deposits by Mr. F.

Ellershausen; and it is understood that well-defined and promising veins have been found.

On the Gillis Lake Road, an excavation made by Mr. J. McKenzie, of Sydney, disclosed a soft, sectile, soapy rock, impregnated with calcspar, drused with a talcose hematite, and holding iron and copper pyrites and green carbonate, in a compact gray and pink felsite. Similar ores occur at other places, as at Boisdale and Coxheath Hills, but have not yet been tested sufficiently to allow of estimates of their value.

At Cheticamp, about 15 years ago, a good deal of work was done on a vein 5 inches thick, holding chrysocolla, blue and green carbonates and grey ores, but the results were presumably unsatisfactory. During the fall of 1879 fresh discoveries of a number of small veins holding copper pyrites were reported from this locality; but owing to the prevailing neglect displayed in making returns by those holding licenses from the crown, I can give no details. At numerous other points, especially in the vicinity of Cape North, the northern part of the Island, specimens of copper ore are found, but no work has been done to test their value.

Although in this Province no copper mines have yet been systematically worked, and many of the deposits have not repaid the prospectors' labour, the indications are so wide spread, and many parts so well adapted, geologically speaking, for workable copper lodes, that we may reasonably expect to see it form a regular article of export before many years. And so long as so many promising indications are met, there will always be an inducement to test their adaptability for working.

In this connection, the presence in the province of the equivalents of the well-known copper bearing strata of Cambrian (?) age, as found in the Province of Quebec, is important. A full description of these strata, their associates, and the manner of occurrence of the ores, will be found in Sir W. Logan's "Geology of Canada," 1863; and they are noticed in subsequent reports of the Survey. This is another of the reasons that could be brought forward as showing the importance of a complete Geological Survey of the Province. The determination and mapping of the great rock series, which hold their peculiar minerals and ores, is a work that every country is now recognizing as due to those who venture their time and money in the development of its mineral resources.

The present tariff imposes a duty of 30 per cent. on manufactures of copper, and of 10 per cent. on the metal. The effect of this has been seen in the impetus given to the copper miners and smelters of Quebec; and it would prove a serviceable assistance to any who were disposed to enter upon such operations in this Province. In this connection, it may be interesting to give the following report of the last ore ticketing of the year 1879, at Swansea:

2109 tons of ore were sold, realising 12,164*l*. 18s. The particulars of the sale were—Average standard for 9 per cent. produce, 91*l*. 1s. 10d.; average produce, 8¾; average price per ton, 5*l*. 15s. 4d.; quantity of fine copper, 186 tons 15½ cwts. The following are the particulars of the two last sales:

Date.	Tons.	Standard.	Produce.	Per ton.	Per unit.	Ore copper.
Nov. 25	1847	£90 19 2	10⅛	£7 2 4	13s. 3 d.	£66 10 5
Dec. 16	2109	91 1 10	8¾	5 15 4	13 0¼	65 2 7

Compared with the last sale, the standard is about stationary, the rise being only 2s. 8d., which scarcely affects the value of the ore. Messrs. Richardson & Co. report that the Betts Cove ore gave a produce of 7⅞ and realised 13s. 2¼d. per unit; Caveira, produce 8 11-16th, per unit 12s. 7¾d.. Union, produce 9¾, per unit 13s.. Berehaven, produce 8⅛, per unit 13s. 9¾d.

LEAD AND SILVER.

The chief ore of lead found in this Province, is Galena, which occurs widely scattered in rocks of every age. It occurs as a very common accessory mineral, with other sulphides, in the auriferous lodes of the Atlantic coast. In this connection it sometimes holds silver up to 6 or 8 ozs. to the ton of ore. Nowhere, however, does it occur in these veins in quantity sufficient to make it valuable by itself.

In the limestones of the Lower Carboniferous, it frequently occurs as disseminated crystals, as at Springville and West River, Pictou County, in Cumberland and other places.

At Gay's River, Halifax County, it is found in this connection in quantities which have warranted somewhat extensive expenditures. The bed rock consists of layers of limestone lying horizontally on the unconformable Silurian slate, and are supposed to be on the same range as the auriferous conglomerate already noticed in this district.

The Galena is found in small crystals scattered through the beds, aggregated about small cavities, and occasionally occurs in small strings. The discovery was first made by the farmers burning the stone for lime, but the explorations continued since that time have not succeeded in finding the ore sufficiently concentrated for working.

Wherever opened, the limestone seems equally charged with Galena at all points in the beds, hundreds of feet apart. The deposit is accessible by simple quarrying, and an abundant supply could be calculated on were any process known capable of treating such a small per centage of ore. Hand specimens can be found giving 17 per cent., but sorting is required to give an average of three per cent. Assays have shown silver to be present in quantities varying from 3 to 12 ounces to the ton of lead.

At Pembroke, in Colchester County, in limestones of similar age, extending over several miles of country, Galena is found everywhere in veins 2 or 3 inches wide and in disseminated crystals. Some prospecting of an irregular character has been done, but little is really known of the deposit. As the ore is more concentrated, this locality offers a better prospect of success than Gay's River.

In this connection it is interesting to recall the fact that in England and other countries extensive mines of lead ore have been opened up in limestones of the same age as those noticed above. This fact lends an importance to the presence of such deposits in this Province; although it must be borne in mind that our limestones are not usually as massive as those of England. A sample of Galena from Musquodoboit, locality not named, gave me on assay 73·56 per cent. of lead.

In Guysborough County, at Caledonia, a vein of Galena, varying in thickness from 1 to 6 inches, was recently tested. Some 16 tons were shipped, but work was stopped, for the ore, although excellent, was not present in quantity large enough to pay the cost of prospecting. The following analysis is from Mr. Poole's Report, 1875:

	No. 1.	No. 2.
Lead	86·12	86·02
*Silver	·044	·049
Iron	·07	·02
Copper	·03	·03
Zinc	Absent	Absent
Arsenic	Mere trace	Mere trace
Antimony	Mere trace	Mere trace
Sulphur	13·32	13·30
Lime	Trace	Trace
Magnesia	Trace	.18
Silica, (sand)	·426	.402
Moisture	Trace	Trace
	100·00	100·00
*Equal to per ton	15·75 oz.	17·75 oz.

Doubtless the district contains other and larger veins carrying Galena, and judging by the samples shown, it offers a fair field to the prospector.

Similar indications of Galena are found in limestones near Sydney and Arichat; and at Port Hood it has been found in a vein in sandstones between two seams of coal, similarly to the Galena at the Joggins, which occurred in a fault. The latter on analysis yielded but two traces of silver.

On the Salmon River Road, near the L'Ardoise Road, Galena and crystals of Calcspar occur in a dark grey fossiliferous limestone. Baddeck, McKenzie, Fishpond Rivers, Guysborough, and other localities are known to yield promising samples of the ore. During 1879 discoveries of Galena, carrying in some cases 100 ounces of silver to the ton, were reported from the head waters of the Gold and LaHave Rivers, but no work has yet been done to allow of any definite statements.

Mr. Fletcher, in the G. S. R. 1876-77, p. 451, states: The value of the quartz veins of the schistose rocks of Burnt and Boulaceet Harbors was tested some years ago by Mr. A. Cameron, of Baddeck. At the former place a number of irregular ferriginous quartz veins, the largest about 15 inches thick, hold traces of argentiferous silver, copper and iron pyrites. An analysis of Dr. Hayes, of a sample from one of the veins showed it to contain 39 oz. 10 dwt. 12 grs. of silver to the ton. At the latter place a vein, from one to four inches thick, cuts the strike of the rocks nearly at right angles. In this was found a large pocket of Galena, holding gold, sulphide of silver, copper and iron pyrites, and producing 18 oz. 9 dwts. 3 grs. of gold, and 97 oz. 10 dwts. 14 grs. silver to the ton. A considerable per-centage of copper pyrites and specular ore is scattered through the hornblendic or quartzose rocks holding the vein.

Between the Upper Settlement of North River and the road from McDonald's Pond to St. Anne's are numerous small quartz veins holding Galena, copper and iron pyrites, and black, honey-colored blende. They appear to form fissures in the red syenite, and to run out or merge gradually into it.

On McDonald's farm, one mile north of the bridge over North River, at the head of tide water, a similar deposit was tested a few years ago. An ill-defined vein, varying in thickness from 3 to 12 inches, composed of quartz carrying galena, copper pyrites and blende, occurs in a greenish, jointed, prophyritic felsite. The junction with the hanging wall was well marked, but the lower and most productive portion of the lode adheres strongly to the foot-wall. A sample of 900 lbs. of the ore yielded, in Boston, 155 lbs. of pig lead and 2·95 oz. of silver to the ton of ore. This district has been represented, by practical miners, as worthy of an extended search, as promising samples of ore have been found at several places in the vicinity.

Silver Ores.—In this connection, it may be mentioned that Mr. Campbell reported discoveries of native silver and its carbonate in veins of soft spar on the McKenzie River, of Inverness Co., Cape Breton, and Mr. Barnes also reported finding it very abundantly in the drift of the same stream. But since the date of their reports, nearly 20 years ago, no further discoveries have been reported. The district lying north of Bras d'Or Lake has been seldom traversed by the mining engineer, and still remains an interesting lone land. From the numerous reports of copper, lead, silver and gold found in the streams running from its high lands, it would afford a promising field to the prospector. From the preceding notes it will be seen that while there are favorable indications of the presence of silver-lead ores, almost no work has been done in the attempt to prove their value. The lower carboniferous limestones in this Province cover a large extent of ground, and may reasonably be expected to afford workable deposits at favorable points—for instance, in proximity to intrusive rocks of later date, or wherever they appear to have been previously in a position favorable to the concentration and deposition of such ores by aqueous agencies.

The geology of Cornwall is duplicated in parts of this Province, and the indications are not wanting of a similar store of mineral wealth. It must be remembered that our woods and snow-laden winters prove an obstacle to the industry of the prospector, and that few among our farmers and fishermen are acquainted with the appearance and form of even the more common ores. I have several times received samples of lead ore, said to have been found in the centre of the western part of the Province, but I am unable to give any details of the localities. These indications are borne out by the discoveries, already alluded to, said to have been made during the past summer. Further developments will prove interesting, for geologically speaking, the localities of the discoveries have been well chosen.

ANTIMONY, MOLYBDENUM, NICKEL AND COBALT, BLENDE, TIN.

Antimony.—This ore is as yet unknown in this Province, except as reported to have been noticed in auriferous quartz lodes. In New

Brunswick, the sulphide of this metal has been found at several places, and I believe a considerable quantity has been exported at various times. As the Silurian strata holding this ore in the neighboring Province are also believed to form part of the pre-carboniferous systems of Nova Scotia, a reasonable expectation may be held out of their occurrence here also.

For the information of those who have not seen the ores of this metal, or are not familiar with its appearance, I give the following description from Danas' Mineralogy of the sulphide, the ore from which the antimony of commerce is obtained : Color and powder, lead grey ; lustre shining, and liable to tarnish. Brittle, but sometimes the thin layers are a little flexible. Generally massive, or semi-fibrous. About four and a half times as heavy as water. About the same hardness as white gypsum or rock salt. It fuses readily in the flame of a candle. Antimony is extensively used in type metal, Britannia ware, pharmaceutical preparations, etc.

Molybdenum.—The sulphide of this metal is found at several places in the Province, as at Gabarus and Louisburg, in Cape Breton, where it occurs in small quantities, over a large extent of country. Hammond's Plains, Lower Musquodoboit, and Lunenburg are also said to have yielded specimens. I am not aware that there is any great demand for it, as, although it can be utilised for several processes in dyeing and coloring, its supply in regular quantities cannot be depended on.

Nickel and Cobalt.—These ores are very common in the Province, but are seldom found in more than traces. Cobalt occurs in mispickel, at Montagu, and I have observed it in the same mineral at Cochran's Hill, Guysborough Co.. Dr. Dawson also shows its presence in copper ore from Carribou, Pictou Co. An analysis of pyrite, from Londonderry Iron Mines, G. S. R. 1874-5, p. 316, gave, when dried at 100° C. :

Iron	45·193
Nickel	·144
Cobalt	·813
Copper	trace
Sulphur	52·434
Silica	·523
Alumina	·513
Ferrous oxide	·179
Lime	·430
Magnesia	·177
	100·406

Dr. How has detected these metals in magnesia alum from Newport, and in magnetic iron pyrites from Nictaux and Geyser's Hill.* Cobalt is frequently found in wad (or bog manganese), and as this compound is very common in the Province, some of the deposits may present it, as a process of concentration, in quantities of economic value.

The mines of Tilt Cove at one time yielded large quantities of nickel pyrites (millerite), which is reported to have frequently brought $675 a ton in England, where the price per pound is now about fifty cents. This ore, I believe, has never been observed in this Province. Nickel is best known in the arts as an alloy, and is extensively used for plating. Cobalt is chiefly used for painting porcelain, pottery, etc. The mineral returns of England gave 98·9 tons of cobalt as the produce of the Kingdom in 1878.

Zinc as yet has been observed in Nova Scotia only as an accessory mineral in auriferous quartz lodes.

Tin.—Messrs. Barnes & Campbell reported finding tinstone at Tangier and Shelburne, associated with decomposed granite debris. I have had specimens brought to me from the neighbourhood of Tangier and Country Harbor. Should this ore prove abundant in the Province, it would form a most valuable adjunct to our mineral resources.

As tinstone is not readily recognized, and specimens have seldom been seen here, I venture to give the following description, which may be useful: But one ore of tin has any commercial value—the oxide, containing when pure, 78 per cent. of the metal. It occurs in modified square prisms, massive or in grains. Its color is brown or black, with adamantine lustre when in crystals, and nearly transparent to opaque. Its powder is pale grey to brownish. It can be scratched slightly by quartz, and gives a light brown or reddish powder, and is from 6 to 7 times as heavy as water. It bears some resemblance to zinc blende (Black Jack), but is harder. Stream tin is the name given to the ore when found in alluvial washings; it is also called wood tin when in a fibrous form. The ore occurs in the crystalline rocks, granite, gneiss, and mica slate.

In Cornwall, the lodes generally run east and west, but are irregular, sometimes crossing one another, or spreading into a network of small veins, or in a flat bed, or in fine crystals disseminated through the rock. The veins are considered worth working when but three inches wide.

* Notes of Pyrrhotites containing nickel, H. How, Mineralogical Magazine, 1877.

Much of the tin is got from loose pieces, accumulated in gravels from the worn down rock, and worked similarly to gold alluvions. The return of the English tin mines for 1878 is said to be:

Tin ore dressed (black tin).......................... 13,632 tons.
" partly dressed (holding 97¼ tons black tin)...... 950 "
" undressed (holding 490¼ tons black tin)......... 9,847 "

CHAPTER III.

MINERALS APPLICABLE TO CERTAIN CHEMICAL MANUFACTURES, ETC.—SULPHUR AND ARSENIC ORES.—CELESTINE.—MANGANESE.

Arsenic.—The most abundant ore of this metal, found in Nova Scotia, is the mispickel or arsenical iron pyrites of the auriferous lodes. Were the demand large enough in Canada, it could be readily made from this mineral, which contains 40 per cent. of it; and the residues, gold, nickel, etc., would be utilized. In various forms the metal is largely used in colouring and other chemical processes. In 1878, 4,464 tons of arsenic, and 3,638 tons of arsenical pyrites were obtained from the mines of England and Ireland.

Sulphur is similarly obtained from sulphurets of iron and copper. Its manufacture has been carried on in Quebec to some extent, but the market is almost entirely supplied with its various compounds from England. The common and magnetic iron pyrites is found frequently in the gold bearing lodes, and scattered through all parts of the Province in rocks of every age. The Lower Silurian (?) slates of Queen's and Lunenburgh Counties frequently show masses and aggregates of crystals, that may lead to deposits of workable size. A large amount of sulphur ores are imported into England, and the produce of iron pyrites in 1878 is given at 14,759 tons. Mr. H. Louis, in a communication to the Nova Scotia Institute of Natural Science, notices its occurrence as crystals in gypsum, near Brookfield, but the amount present was not large.

From the Catalogue of Canadian Minerals at the Philadelphia Exhibition, it appears that in 1875 the manufacture of sulphuric and muriatic acids was commenced at Elizabethtown. The pyrites comes from a large deposit associated with quartzites and gneises of Laurentian age; and yields about 40 per cent of sulphur, and a ton of pyrites produces nearly a ton of acid. The capacity of the works is three tons of acid (66° Baume) daily.

Celestine.—This mineral was noticed by Mr. Fletcher, in Cape Breton, G. S. R., 1875-6 6, p. 417, who states that it is found on the right bank of Sydney river, about a mile and a half above the bridge, where a bluish gray bed about a foot in thickness, containing specks of galena, may be seen for a considerable distance along the river, overlaid by gray, slatey limestone. This mineral is one of the sources of the nitrate of Strontium used for the production of red fire in pyrotechny.

Manganese Ores.—These ores are very common in this Province, as pyrolusite, psilomane, manganite, and bog manganese. They are as yet known in workable quantities only in the limestones of the Lower Carboniferous age. Traces of the ores have been met in these strata wherever they occur, especially in Cumberland, Pictou, Colchester, Hants and Kings Counties, in nodules and strings up to a few pounds in weight. I have observed it near the Pictou iron deposits in masses weighing up to 200 lbs.

In Hants County, these ores have received a good deal of attention, and an irregular annual export has been maintained, amounting since 1861, to about 2,000 tons, valued at $110,000. Here it occurs as pyrolusite, with manganite, a little limonite, barytes and calcspar, in nodules in the soil, and as pockets and irregular layers in the limestone. The deposits are said to extend over the whole Lower Carboniferous district of the County wherever the lower limestones are exposed. The ores have been followed to a depth of 75 feet, and the limestones holding them are said to be 300 feet thick.

Quite extensive operations were carried on at Teny Cape, Walton and Pembroke, for a number of years, but are at present continued only by Mr. J. Stephens, of Teny Cape, who shipped, last year, 90 tons of first-class ore, valued at $4,950, and 55 tons of second-class ore, valued at $2,220. These Hants County ores are frequently very high class, yielding from 90 per cent. and upwards of peroxide, and containing but traces of iron. This ore is employed by the flint glass maker for correcting the greenish tinge given to glass by the iron present in the sand; consequently, he values it in proportion to its freedom from this ingredient. This and the sesquioxide or manganite are also used in making chloride of lime, glass pastes, black enamel for pottery, tiles, etc. Other forms are used in calico printing and many industrial applications. It is well known as a valuable ingredient in certain ores of iron largely imported into England for steel making, etc., and its presence in some of the Pictou ores already alluded to. For many of the above purposes, ores holding as low as 35 per cent. of oxide are available, and much of that imported into England is not of a higher per-cent. The amount raised in England in 1878 was 1,734 tons, valued at about £3 13 6 per ton. The amount imported in 1876 was 8,914 tons, valued at £44,659, and from £2 10 to £13 per ton. In Onslow, Colchester County, about 6 miles from Truro, it has been found in limestones similar to those of Teny Cape, extending from Little's farm to the Salmon River, and is believed to be present in workable quantities. In Pictou County, on the East and Middle Rivers, it is present to a considerable extent as carbonate in the limestones, and on search, may be found concentrated as an oxidysed residue in quantity sufficient for working. As the district in Hants County, above alluded to as yielding promising indications of the leading ores, is over 150 square miles in extent, it will be seen that the present out-put is limited more by want of enterprise or interest than by any probable deficiency of the ore. I am not aware that these ores have been reported from any part of Cape Breton, nor has Mr. Fletcher noticed them in his surveys, which have embraced the greater part of the carboniferous formation of that Island.

Dr. How, in a paper read before the N. S. I. N. S., in 1865, gave the following table of manganese per-centages:

Manganite.	Cheverie, Hants Co........p. c.	47·73
Wad.	Halifax Co...............	56·00
Pyrolusite.	Douglas, Hants Co........	84·62
"	Teny Cape, "	88·01
"	" "	92·69
"	" "	95·00
"	Cumberland Co...........	97.04

Bog Manganese.—This is the name given to those common swamp mineral concentrations which are iron or manganese ores, as one or the other compound predominates. They also hold clay, lime, magnesia, salt and sometimes cobalt and copper. The color of the wads or manganiferous deposits varies from black to light brown, and they are generally broken without any difficulty. Analyses of the bog iron ores have been already given. The following is an analysis by myself of a wad found in a large bed on Boularderie Island, Cape Breton :

Oxide of Manganese........................	44·33
" Iron............................	35·50
Silicious Residue...........................	1·00
Lime and Magnesia........................	
Water, Carbonaceous Matter, etc..............	18·23
	99·56

These compounds are generally known as paints, and are allied to the ochres formed by the decomposition of limestones holding iron and manganese. Dr. How reported finding in the brown paint from Bridgewater, Lunenburg Co., 11 per cent. of manganese. Other localities are Chester, Parrsborough, Jeddore, Beech Hill, Lochaber, Tracadie, Louisburg, Sydney, etc.

The total exports of Manganese from Canada for the year 1877-8 were 1,066 tons, of which New Brunswick sent 956 tons, valued at $12,452. From this it would appear that the New Brunswick ores are of comparatively low grades, while those from Hants Co. are equal in value to the average high grade ores imported into England.

Were the manganite and pysolusite deposits of this Province tested and carefully prepared for shipment, there is no doubt, from the large extent of country yielding them, that they could be made a profitable article of export. The writer is indebted to Mr. Blackwell, of 26 Chapel Street, Liverpool, an extensive dealer, for much information relative to the market value of Nova Scotian and other Manganese ores.

CHAPTER IV.

MINERAL MANURES.—GYPSUM.—PHOSPHATES.

Gypsum.—This mineral is known in the Province under two forms, as soft gypsum, containing:

Lime	32·55
Sulphuric Acid	46·51
Water	20·94

and as hard gypsum, or anhydrite, which consists of 41 per cent. of lime and 59 per cent. of sulphuric acid. The mineral is found in extensive beds, varying in thickness from a few inches up to 120 feet, and also occurs disseminated in fine grains in the shales, marls and limestones which are usually associated with it. In the Maritime Provinces it occurs in the Lower or Marine Carboniferous formation, already referred to in connection with the manganese ores, and where the limestones appear it is usually at no great distance. Its appearance is so well known, and it is so widely scattered through the northern and eastern part of the Province, that a catalogue of its exposures would be an endless task and serve no useful purpose. The chief localities yielding it are Windsor, Cheverie, Maitland, Walton, Hantsport, Wallace, Antigonish, Mabou, Judique, Port Hood, Port Hawkesbury, and many places on the Bras d'Or Lake, and in Pictou County.

So far as known, it occurs at no fixed horizon in the Marine Limestone formation; being found at Sydney, a few feet below the Millstone Grit, and in Pictou County almost in contact with Silurian strata. Among the minerals found in the gypsum may be mentioned glauber salt, common salt, calcspar, magnesium carbonate, arragonite, carbonate and oxide of iron, silica, and free sulphur. The late Dr. How also discovered the following interesting minerals, which, if found in quantity, would prove very valuable. They are compounds of borax occurring in the gypsum and anhydrite of the Windsor district, and are presented in crystals and nodules up to 2 in. in diameter; in some cases forming a considerable per centage of the rock. The nodules are sometimes pearly white, compact and hard; in other specimens they are made up of accicular tufts of prismatic crystals, colorless and translucent. The following table shows the composition of these minerals, and also of another discovered by the same gentleman at a later date, and apparently formed by partial replacement of the Ulexite by Selenite. The Ulexite is a very pure form of the Peruvian borate "Tiza," which is found, I believe, only in these two countries. It has been largely exported into England and the United States from Peru, for the manufacture of borax and for use in glazing operations. Should these deposits be found to occur in quantity, it would form a valuable export, and materially aid the out-put of the associated gypsum.

	Natroboro calcite Ulexite Dana.	Cryptomor- phite.	Silicoboro calcite Howlite Dana.	Wink- worthite.
Water............	34·49	19·74	11·84	18·00
Lime.............	14·20	14·50	28·69	31·14
Sulphuric acid.....	.....	.....	.....	31·51
Silicic "	.....	.....	15·25	4·98
Boracic " ...	44·10	59·10	42·22	14·37
Soda............	14·20	5·68	.....	.....
	100·00	100·00		

The deposits of gypsum in Nova Scotia are on an unequalled scale; the beds are frequently traceable for miles by exposures presenting faces 50 feet in thickness. In Antigonish it occurs on St. George's Bay, as a crystalline cliff 200 feet high, and similar exposures are met at Plaster Cove, Mabou, and many places on the Bras d'Or. This scale of exposure, and the frequent proximity of the deposits to good shipping places, has materially aided its output. The facilities for quarrying have allowed its extraction at rates varying from 45c. to 65c. a ton, and this low price can be maintained for many years to come.

The anhydrite is found as lenticular masses of every size imbedded in the gypsum, and as beds underlying and alternating with it. The soft gypsum, however, is the one chiefly quarried. It has been largely exported in the raw form to the United States, where it is ground for a fertiliser, or boiled and ground for finishing houses, cornices, mouldings, etc., according to its pureness and color. It is said to be a suitable dressing for tobacco and cotton lands, and large quantities are mined for this purpose in Saltville, Virginia.

Ontario annually imports from the States about $20,000 worth of ground Nova Scotia gypsum for top-dressing, in addition to that furnished by the gypsum beds of the Onondaga period, in the vicinity of the Grand River.

As a prohibitive duty is imposed on ground gypsum imported into the States, we are unable to pursue the manufacture of the plaster for their markets, but are obliged to furnish them with the raw material only. Thus New Brunswick sends only about $2,000 of ground gypsum to the United States, and none is exported by Nova Scotia. This is very much to be regretted, as the value of say 25,000 tons of ground gypsum would be about $113,000, or more than the value of an export of five times that amount of the raw material.

At Hillsborough, in New Brunswick, there is a large plaster mill which supplies the local demands with a very superior article. At this establishment a 40 horse power engine furnishes the power necessary for driving the stones, working pans, making barrels, etc. Four cauldrons are used, each holding 18,000 ℔s.; in the course of the day, each will yield three charges. At present this mill is working at only one-fifth of its capacity.

From information, kindly furnished by the manager, it appears that the cost of the calcined gypsum, is about 90 cts. per barrel of 300 ℔s (including barrel and paper.) This cost would be materially reduced if the mill were working to its full capacity. The Nova Scotia plaster sells at $1·86, and the Hillsborough at 2·00 a barrel in Halifax. A considerable quantity of gypsum is prepared for agricultural purposes in the Province, although, as the farming districts are chiefly in the carboniferous measures, nature has already supplied it in many places. There are a number of small local mills where the gypsum is ground for architectural purposes, but no account can be got of the amounts thus utilised. Last year Walton shipped 50 tons of ground gypsum, valued at $225.

It may be remarked that at many points in the Province, as Antigonish and Windsor, the transparent, pure variety of gypsum, commonly called isinglass, and known to the mineralogist as Selenite, can be procured in large quantity, and also almost chemically pure, massive, white gypsum. These qualities are specially utilised for cornices and centre-pieces, and when they can be regularly obtained, furnish the best material for the more common applications of the manufactured article.

The anhydrite has hitherto been utilised for few purposes; it is quite as well adapted for agricultural use as the soft gypsum, but as it requires stamping for its pulverisation, its cost is thereby increased over that of the other, which can be readily ground. It has been used for foundation walls, etc., but is not durable enough for any permanent building purposes. It takes a good polish, and has several times been cut for mantels, table tops, etc., but has not come into general use, as it is believed not to stand exposure long enough to supplant marble. The following statistics will show the extent of the trade which has been carried on for many years—

Quantity and value of gypsum exported from Nova Scotia:

	Tons.	Value.
1855	95,301	$ 80,875
1860	105,431	85,936
1865	56,155	45,088
1870	98,050	75,650
1873	120,693	120,693

In the year ending June 30, 1877, Canada exported 101,376 tons, of which Nova Scotia furnished 96,440 tons, valued at $89,488; and in 1878, 101,134 tons were exported from Canada, of which Nova Scotia furnished 94,607 tons, valued at $85,049. The amount exported from Nova Scotia during the year 1879 was 95,126 tons, valued at $74,923. The total exports from Nova Scotia since 1854 are, so far as my information goes, about 2,300,000, valued at about $1,900,000. The total amount shipped from Windsor since 1833 is approximately 2,544,376 long tons, valued at about $2,000,000. Mr. Hunt gives the quantity raised in England in 1878 at 74,908 tons, valued at $109,438.

Were any revision of our present tariff arrangements with the United States carried out, and the duty on the manufactured article taken off, the plaster trade would assume important dimensions in Hants County, and the export would be correspondingly increased by the reduced prices.

Phosphatic Nodules.—Mr. H. Fletcher, G. S. R. 1876-7, p. 433, mentions finding in the Lower Silurian Limestones of Mackintosh Brook, Cape Breton, layers of phosphatic nodules. Similar nodules are not uncommon in Quebec, and have been observed at Arisaig and in Colchester County, samples from the River Ouelle having yielded upwards of 40 per cent. of phosphate of lime. The Cape Breton deposits are not considered of economic value; but were they in any quantity, a valuable fertiliser could be manufactured for local use.

CHAPTER V.

MINERAL PIGMENTS.—BARYTES.—OCHRES.

Paints.—This name may be applied to two classes of mineral aggregations found in this Province. The first consists essentially of iron ores, composed of hydrated peroxide of iron, with manganese, silica, alumina, and water of hydration. They are frequently, as far as their composition goes, valuable ores of iron, being originally carbonates of lime, iron, and magnesia, in varying proportions, and having lost, by infiltration, the lime, phosphates, and the sulphur compounds, and much of the magnesia. But, owing to their large per-centages of moisture, and friable nature, they cannot be utilised for the blast furnace, unless first made into briquettes. Good examples of these classes of paints are to be met at the Londonderry Iron Mines, where they appear to have been derived from the Ankerite and Sideroplesite forming the vein stone. The following analyses show the original and present composition of these minerals:

COMPOSITION.	ANKERITES.			OCHRES.	
	Yellow.	Brown.		Yellow.	Red.
Iron—Carbonate	23·45	20·30	Peroxide	74·52	70·20
Lime—Carbonate	43·80	49·20		·40	5·50
Magnesia—Carbonate	30·80	30·20	....		2·80
Manganese—Carbonate	·80	....	Oxide	....	·45
Silica	·10	....	....	6·20	14·40
Alumina	....	....	....	4·80	6·80
Water	....	....	....	14·40	....

The red colors produced by burning the ochres are modified to purples by manganese, and to browns and greys by mixtures of white clay and other impurities. Similar ochres occur in Antigonish and Pictou Counties in connection with the specular ore veins, and at Chester and numerous other points. At Chester the ochres are formed by the oxidation and hydration of the limestones of the Lower Carboniferous age, and frequently contain large quantities of manganese, affording purplish paints which were formerly manufactured to a considerable extent, and are still used locally.

The other classes of ochres have been formed by water depositing in beds of earth, marl, etc., oxides of iron, manganese, etc. Such deposits occur at Folly Mountain, Onslow, Kentville, Cornwallis, Polson's Lake, Chezzetcook, Lunenburg, and many places in Cape Breton. As already mentioned, these last-named ochres pass insensibly into bog iron ores and wad manganese, accordingly as the oxide of iron or manganese predominates.

Considerable quantities of ochres are prepared in the Province of Quebec, but the imports and exports of this article are small. The quantity of ochre raised in England during the year 1878 was 2,903 tons, chiefly from Anglesea, and worth, on an average, £1 2s. 6d. per ton of 2,240 lbs.

Messrs. Brandram Bros., of Rotherhithe, S. E., near London, write : "Scarcely any ochres are available as pigments until they have been very finely cleansed and levigated, and then very much depends upon their staining power as well as the richness of their color, and this is in some cases more valuable when they have been carefully and thoroughly burned, as with the Italian Terra de Sienna, Turkey Umber, and others known as metallic oxides. The ochres most in demand here are from the mines in Wales, and also from those in Auxerre, in France, and they vary in value from £2 10s. to £12 per ton of 2240 lbs. The French ochres are prepared and levigated before they are sent to this country, and are mostly in an impalpable powder. Those from Italy are in lumps, as is also a celebrated yellow ochre, known as Oxford stone ochre, found in Oxfordshire. The writer remembers to have seen some very fine ochres in Nova Scotia in 1876, but at that time no care or trouble had been taken in their preparation, and he is of opinion that it would be useless to send them to Europe until this had been done."

Barytes.—This mineral, generally known as "heavy spar," is frequently met in this Province. It is confined to no particular horizon in the geological sequence, but occurs in the Carboniferous, and all the older strata. It is extensively used as an adulterant for paints and enamels, etc. In England the amount raised in 1878 is put down at 21,715 tons, valued at about £21,000. The mineral sells in proportion to its freedom from iron, copper and other ores, imparting a color to the ground material. Other impurities, such as silica, gypsum, etc., are not so injurious.

At Five Islands, Colchester County, it occurs in irregular pockets in the Lower Carboniferous. The mineral is frequently in the beautiful characteristic tabular crystals, and is associated with calcspar and copper pyrites. About 1000 tons have been exported to the United States, and a considerable quantity manufactured for home use. Some years ago a few hundred tons were mined from veins in Lower Carboniferous sandstones and shales on the Stewiacke River, near Brookfield.

During the last few years this mineral has been intermittently mined at River John, where it occurs in veins, in measures said to be of Lower Carboniferous age. The quantity exported from River John in 1879 amounted to 480 tons, valued at $2,400. It also occurs associated with limonite at the mouth of the Shubenacadie River and Clifton, and at Brookfield, near the iron ores of that locality. Among other localities may be mentioned the Lower Carboniferous of the Avon, Musquodoboit and Wallace Rivers, and Greenville, Cumberland County. It is frequently found with the manganese ores of Hants and Colchester Counties. I have also seen samples from Antigonish County, Whyhogomah, Cheticamp, Loch Lomond, St. Annes and other Cape Breton localities. Although occurring in numerous places, it is the exception to find the ore holding only traces of impurity.

CHAPTER VI.

SALT.—MINERAL WATERS.

Salt.—This mineral in many countries is intimately connected with gypsums and marls, in rocks of various ages.

Salt is found in crystals in many of our gypsum quarries, and springs holding large quantities of it issue from their neighborhood. As yet, however, no bed of salt has been found in this Province. The importance of a discovery of such deposits may be gathered from the fact that during the year 1877-8, Nova Scotia imported for home consumption, 930,114 bushels of salt, valued at $99,392, and last year's importation was valued at $105,207. England made in 1878 1,500,000 tons of white salt from brine, and 182,930 tons of rock salt.

No systematic test has ever yet been made of our gypsums and marls at a proper depth from the surface, and the subject is one worthy of serious attention. In Goderich, Ontario, extensive beds of rock salt were discovered in 1866, in deposits, in many points identical with our Marine Limestone formation, but of much greater age. An interesting account of these discoveries will be found in the G. S. R., 1876-7, and elsewhere. From Mr. Smith's Report, 1874-5, it appears that in 1873, 451,576 barrels of salt were made, and valued at $436,217. In 1876-7, Canada exported 789,599 bushels, valued at $82,323.

In Nova Scotia, salt has been made at various times from brine springs, and in some cases a superior quality was produced, but at present very little is being done. Among the various springs, the best known are those of Renfrew, Walton, Salt Springs, and Irish Mountain, Pictou County, Sutherland's River, Antigonish, Ohio, Baddeck, Whyhogomah, River Philip and Black Brook, Cumberland County. At the last named locality, salt is at present manufactured by the Messrs. Gilroy, and is suitable for house use. The following analyses will show the character of some of these brine springs:

	Walton.	West River.	Bras d'Or. Little Narrows.
Lime Carbonate	14·73	3·775	.....
Magnesia "	traces	2·932	.....
Iron "	"	.....	.....
Phosphoric Acid	"	.....	.....
Magnesium Chloride	4·48	27·330	.1593
Lime Sulphate	161·16	154·730	5·6810
Common Salt	787·11	4133·500	50·6881
Silica	.....	·560	trace
Calcium Chloride	.....	51·910	·1942
Total	967·48	4374·917	56·7226
Salt per cent	1·1	5·9	....

The analyses of the Walton and West River brines are by the late Dr. How, and give the contents in grains to the imperial gallon; that of the Bras d'Or Spring, is from the G. S. R., p. 181, 1873-4, and gives the solid contents in 1000 parts.

MINERAL WATERS OF NOVA SCOTIA.

There are numerous mineral springs in Nova Scotia, as would be expected from the variety of its geological formations, and the deep-seated disturbances which have brought them to the surface. Many of these springs are locally believed to exercise healing or restorative powers, and in some cases it appears justly so. Others again owe their fame merely to an abnormal taste, caused by common salts not present in quantities large enough to exert medicinal effects. The late Dr. How examined several of these waters. The results of his labors, and a few analyses by the writer and the chemist of the Geological Survey, comprise all that is positively known about them. In the event of a Geological Survey being extended over the Province, these springs merit a careful examination, as the presence of mineral waters of undoubted excellence has frequently done much to attract tourists and visitors, and produce thereby other benefits equally important, although, perhaps, not so conspicuous. Among these springs, that of Wilmot, some fifty years ago, had a considerable reputation, but is now seldom visited. On the property of Mr. Bowman, near Windsor, is a spring rising from the Lower Carboniferous limestones and gypsums, and containing, as would be expected, an unusually large amount of Sulphate of Gypsum.

An Alkaline spring is known near Chester, Lunenburg County. On the Salmon River, in Cape Breton, another spring is known, and reported to have effected cures in rheumatic and asthmatic complaints. The water rises in syenitic rocks, considered to be of Laurentian age. Cheticamp, Mabou, and Grand Anse are other localities yielding mineral waters. Gair Loch, Irish Mountain, Sutherland's River, and Salt Springs are localities in Pictou County, where mineral waters of local repute are known. Earltown, Shelburne, Renfrew, and several other places are also noted for mineral springs, said to be useful in many disorders.

Composition.	Salmon River.	Windsor.	Wilmot.	Bras d'Or Lake.
Iron	traces	......	....	....
Phosphoric Acid	"	trace	trace	....
Carbonate of Lime	} ·60	17·50	2·70	....
" Magnesia		·31	·37	....
" Iron	......	·40	·14	....
Chloride of Sodium	343·11	·90	....	50·68
" Potassium	4·55	....	1·60	·19
" Calcium	308·90	....	....	....
" Magnesium	4·47	....	....	·15
Sulphate of Lime	·94	106·21	121·98	5·68
" Soda	....	·68	8·35	....
" Potash	...	·38	....	....
" Magnesia	....	11·02	5·35	....
Silica	....	·60	·55	traces
Total	*662·57	*138·00	*141·04	† 56·72

In a paper read before the Newcastle-on-Tyne Institute,‡ I referred to the various pit waters met in our coal mines, and gave analyses made by myself and others.

It may be remarked that the composition, sources and effects of the hidden springs of the earth are as yet but little known, but it may be expected that at some future day the composition of mineral springs, and the waters cut by bore-holes, etc., may be brought into the service of man, and furnish valuable information about the proximity of mineral deposits and strata. The following table shows the composition of several of these waters, some of which have been found to exert a highly corrosive effect on all iron exposed to their action, while others are comparatively innocuous.

* Analyst, Dr. How, grns. in Imperial Gal.
† Analyst, Dr. Harrington, in 1000 parts.
‡ Notes on Nova Scotia Pit Waters, E. Gilpin, 1879.

COMPOSITION.	GARDENER COLLIERY.	VALE COLLIERY.	NOVA SCOTIA COLLIERY.	COMPOSITION.	SPRING HILL.
Sulphate of Iron......	2·750	....	....	....	......
" Potassium	·187	....	1·580	....	......
" Magnes'm.	....	1·000	....	....	......
" Calcium ..	....	·514	....	....	......
" Sodium...	....	....	2·500	....	......
Carbonate of Lime....	·736	trace	10·590	Carbonic Acid.	not est:
" Mags'm..	·025	trace	3·570	Alkalies.	6·23
" Sodium..	....	7·509	3·350	Chlorine.	·75
Chloride of Calcium..	....	....	....	Sulphuric Acid.	34·82
" Sodium ..	·960	1·452	1·170	Magnesia.	7·94
" Potassium	....	....	....	Lime.	8·03
Iron Oxides.........	....	trace	....	....	4·08
Alumina.............	trace	....	....	....	·58
Silica....˙.........	·225	·190	·460	....	1·55
Potassium	....	trace	....	....	....
	*4·881	*9·765	*23·220		63·98

* Analyst, E. Gilpin, calculated to 1000 parts.

CHAPTER VII.

MATERIALS APPLICABLE TO BUILDING PURPOSES.—FREESTONES.—GRANITE, ETC.—FLAGS AND SLATES.—CLAY.—LIMESTONES.— MARBLES.— CEMENTS.

Building Stones.—The building stones of Nova Scotia are chiefly sandstones and granites. The various grades of the former are supplied almost entirely from the Upper Coal Measures. We accordingly find the quarries in the Counties of Pictou and Cumberland, and parts of Colchester and Hants. In Pictou, large quarries were in operation some years ago, at the head of Pictou Harbor, and shipped annually about 5000 tons. During the last few years the export trade has been carried on chiefly by Messrs. Hogg & McKeen, who supply an article of first-class quality. Other quarries have been opened at Glenfallock and Middle River. A considerable quantity of stone for the use of the Eastern Counties Railway was quarried at Merigomish Harbor. Every harbor and river from Pictou to Amherst affords building stones, frequently of good quality, as at Wallace and Tatmagouche.

Samples were sent to the Philadelphia Exhibition from a quarry at Wallace, situated about 150 feet above high water mark, and only 600 yards from a good harbor. The beds are horizontal, and for the first fifteen feet from the surface, vary in thickness from four inches to two feet. Below this there is a massive bed which, according to Mr. Heustis, is from three to eight feet thick. It is divided into rectangular masses by joints from six to fourteen feet apart, which greatly facilitates the quarrying. The cost of the stone, delivered on board vessels in the harbor, is from forty to sixty cents per cubic foot.

At the Joggins, Minudie, and River Philip, valuable deposits have been opened. Passing to the Basin of Minas: Cornwallis, Johnston's Brook, Horton, Falmouth, Kennetcook and Old Barns are known to contain material adapted for building purposes.

About half of the stone used in the St. Peter's Canal was from the south-east side of Boularderie Island and the vicinity of Kelly's Cove. The Boularderie quarry was abandoned, owing to the heavy capping. There was also much broken stone in the Kelly Cove quarry; and great part of the material used was from boulders. The locks were finally finished with stone from Wallace, as the engineer in charge did not succeed in finding suitable material on the Bras d'Or Lake.

The reports of the Mines Department give the shipments of freestone for the years 1873-9, at 45,814 tons; the value varying from $2 to $20 per ton.

Syenites, Porphyries and Granites.—Granite is very abundant in the older rocks of the Province. Among localities which have furnished it for building purposes, may be mentioned Shelburne, Queens and Lunenburg Counties. It also occurs at Aspotogen and various points thence to Halifax. As already mentioned, in describing the Gold fields, it runs almost continuously from Halifax to Windsor, and thence westward. It occurs again at Waverley, and runs through Musquodoboit, Jeddore, Ship Harbor, Sherbrooke, and Country Harbor to Canso. It occurs inland at the head waters of many of the Eastern Rivers, and is estimated to cover a large area of the Atlantic district. It has, however, been quarried only at points accessible to shipping. At Halifax, it has been used a good deal about the fortifications, and a number of houses have been constructed of it, its cost, rough, being from $2.25 to $4.00 a ton.

In the Cobequids, there are masses of flesh and red colored Syenite, which have afforded very handsome polished samples; but, as yet, have not been worked for construction. Prophyries and Syenites occur in various parts of Cape Breton, but their economic value has not been tested. The following localities may be mentioned—St. Ann's, Boisdale, and Coxheath. The crystalline diorites of Louisburg were used by the French in building their fortifications.

Limestones.—This material has not been used to any extent in Nova Scotia, for building purposes, although it is frequently found to stand exposure well, and to be readily quarried. Among localities yielding it, may be mentioned the Shubenacadie River, Kennetcook, Lower Horton, Thompson Station; Glengarry and Springville, Pictou County. Stones from a quarry here, retain, after an exposure of forty years, every trace of the chisel or pick. The marbles will be noticed further on.

As before mentioned, the anhydric or hard gypsum has been used to a small extent for walls, foundations, etc. A flaggy arenaceous schist, known as iron stone, was extensively used some years ago, for warehouses and walls in Halifax. Many of the metamorphic sandstones of the Atlantic coast would furnish a most durable and pleasing building material.

At present the supply of wood for building purposes is so plentiful, that brick or stone houses are the exception. Even public buildings, churches, halls, etc., are almost always of wood; but as this material becomes more expensive, the labor of the quarrymen will succeed that of the lumbermen, and our towns become something better than wooden shells, blackened by smoke.

Flags and Slates.—A small amount of flagstone has been quarried on the North West Arm of Halifax Harbor, and at Beaver Bank. Slates were quarried to a small extent at Rawdon, and various places in Hants County, and the quality and quantity are equal to any demand. Dalhousie Mountain and West River, Pictou, are said to have good slate beds, and it is also reported from the South Mountain, Digby, and Yarmouth Counties. At the Provincial Exhibition of 1879, slates were shown from Sackville, River John and Upper Stewiacke, which, although in the rough, were of good material.

The demand for roofing slates will become general in the Province in a few years, as their superiority over the shingles in ordinary use becomes apparent.

Brick Clay.—These clays are found in many places, presenting an unlimited supply of raw material to the brick maker. As yet, brick is but little used in the Province, although when well made and used according to proper designs, it makes the best building material for this climate. The best known clay fields are those of Shubenacadie, along the line of the Intercolonial Railway, and many points in the carboniferous districts of Colchester, Pictou, Cumberland and Antigonish.

The present selling price of brick in Halifax is, for best at Depot, $8.00 per M; Chettezcook $6.00 per M on wharf. The amount of brick imported into Canada during 1876-7 was 2,218 M, valued at $10,823. During 1877-8, it was 1,981 M, valued at $8,213. In 1877-8, Nova Scotia imported 125 M, valued at $768. The present annual make of brick in Nova Scotia cannot be readily estimated, but may be approximated at 10,000 M.

At the Provincial Exhibition of 1879 samples of brick of good quality were exhibited by Messrs. Smith & Kaye, Miller and others.

·It may be remarked that very many of our home-made brick are carelessly made. Proper attention is not always given to the weathering, picking out of pebbles of limestone, etc., and the clay is seldom ground or otherwise divided, and too frequently the proper admixtures of mild earths are not attended to. The life of Nova Scotia bricks is generally far shorter than it should be, as when properly made it is one of the most durable materials known to the architect. The bricks made by the French at Mira, and extensively used in the building of Louisburg, were carefully prepared, and remain at the present day as sound as when they came from the kiln.

Limestones.—In Nova Scotia the limestones are confined practically to the Lower Carboniferous, and are generally associated with the gypsums. There are also beds of this mineral in the Laurentian, etc. of Cape Breton, and in the Cambrian and Silurian measures, but they do not usually form deposits of economic value. The carboniferous limestones are strongly developed in Cumberland, Colchester, Hants, Kings, Pictou and Antigonish Counties, and at many points in Cape Breton. They occur in beds varying in thickness from a few inches to 50 feet, and in some localities their aggregate dimensions will exceed 400 feet. Their quality varies from calcareous sandstones and clays to the almost crystalline pure mineral.

At Windsor, Brookfield, and many other localities beds are found composed entirely of fossils, characterising the Marine Limestone formation, and gave the following component parts on analysis by Dr. How :

Carbonate of Lime	97·64
" Magnesia	1·10
Oxide of Iron	·07
Phosphoric Acid	trace
Insoluble residue	·68

A limestone similar to the above is extensively quarried at Brookfield as a flux for the Londonderry iron ores, the quantity forwarded for this purpose in 1878 and 1879 being about 16,000 tons.

The limestones of Pictou County are also well adapted for fluxes, and will be found useful whenever smelting operations are commenced on the East River. The following analyses of a limestone from Lime Brook, Springville, were made for the Halifax Co. at the Durham College of Physical Science :

	I.	II.
Lime Carbonate	93·90	96·26
Magnesia "	2·45	2·33
Iron Peroxide	·59	·57
Manganese "	·56	·55
Alumina	·12	·10
Sulphur	·03	·02
Phosphoric Acid	·03	·03
Silica	2·10	1·99
Moisture	·18	·17

These results are confirmed by an extensive series of analyses made some years ago by the writer, embracing all the more important exposures of that mineral in the vicinity of the Pictou coal and iron deposits, but the space at my disposal would forbid its insertion. The position of the East River limestones, forms an important item in their adaptability for fluxing purposes; they occur as a band everywhere between the coal and iron, so that their transport becomes a matter of comparatively low cost, and large quantities are available by simple quarry work.

Some limestones at Horton, Onslow, the Joggins, Pugwash and other places are bituminous, and contain notable quantities of phosphoric acid. As already mentioned, some of the East River limestones contain important per-centages of carbonate of iron, and may, at some localities, afford an ore of this metal, in addition to the Spathic ores referred to before.

In Cape Breton, several places are known which afford marbles, believed to be well adapted for building and decorative purposes. The finest deposit of workable limestone yet discovered, is on West Bay, Bras d'Or Lake. In variety of color and tint, this rock resembles the limestones of the George River series, of which it forms a part, but it contains little or no admixture of foreign materials, and is uniform in texture and in unequalled abundance. The following varieties have been recognised:

1. Fine white statuary marble.
2. Fine white building "
3. Coarse white building "
4. Blue and white clouded "
5. Brocatello marble mixed with six varieties of colored marbles.
6. Fine flesh colored marbles, often striped and variegated.

The locality offers every facility for quarrying and shipping, and on the completion of the St. Peters Canal, blocks of any required dimentions can be cheaply shipped to the United States, equal in quality to those already admired as samples.

At St. Anne's Mountain, Cape Dauphin, Salmon Creek, Whyhogomah, River Dennis, George River, French Valley and Escasonie, marbles are also found ; at the latter place they are usually too much broken and mixed with other rock to be available for artistic purposes. At Five Islands, Colchester County, promising marble deposits are known. The carboniferous and other limestones are quarried at all points for lime for building and agricultural purposes. That from East Bay has been extensively burned for lime, as has also that from the George's River beds, which furnished in 1876 about 6,000 barrels, invoiced at 80 cts. a barrel. The Nova Scotia lime is frequently brown, arising probably from carelessness in selecting and burning ; its price per barrel may be averaged at 95 cents. At numerous points in the Province, the limestones contain foreign ingredients, indicating the presence of a certain amount of hydraulicity, such as Alumina, Carbonate of iron, Magnesia, Silica, etc.

The well-known Portland Cement was invented in accordance with the desire for a material which would set rapidly, and remain indurated in water. Lime, itself, is useless for this purpose, unless mixed with the proper proportions of an argillaceous compound. Many good natural cements, such as the Roman Cement, have been used at various times, but the want of uniformity in the composition of the calcareo argillaceous rocks they were made from, soon rendered their action even dangerous.

There are several natural cements still made, resembling the Portland compound in composition and qualities, such as the Boulogne and English Lias, as shown by the following analyses :

	Lime.	Silica.	Alumina.	Iron Oxide.	Magnesia.
Portland Cement..	62·0	23·0	8·00	4·0	...
Boulogne " ..	65·15	20·42	13·87	...	·58

One important difference between the natural and artificial cements, is the shrinkage in setting of the former. This, and the difficulty of preserving uniformity of composition, have gradually led to the almost exclusive use of the artificial cement. The general character of the materials used in the manufacture of Portland Cement may be gathered from the following analyses :*

CHALK—Lime, 56·5   Carbonic Acid, 43·00   Water, ·5
CLAY—Silica, 68·45   Alumina, 11·64   Lime, ·75   Iron
              Oxide, 14·80   Soda, 4·00

* 'Reid—Treatise on Concrete.

The proportions used are from 65 to 75 per cent. of chalk ; and from 25 to 35 per cent. of clay—any kind of chalk being suitable ; but the clay should not contain above 14 per cent. of iron oxides. The process of manufacture, which is too long for proper description here, requires intelligent supervision, to produce an article of uniform quality. In Germany, limestones are used instead of chalk ; but the cement very closely resembles that made in England. In this Province, although many limestones possess hydraulic qualities, their uniformity cannot be relied on. Hence, our cements, which are natural ones, have never proved permanently satisfactory. The limestones and clays of the Province will answer for the manufacture of cement ; but the absence of chalk, requires more care in the manipulation of the limestone, and a consequently increased cost.

The present selling price of Portland Cement, in Halifax, is $4.25 per barrel. The amount imported in 1877-8, was 76,847 barrels, valued at $106,018.00 ; and the importation of last year was valued at $65,832.00. The expense of manufacturing this article in the Province would be considerably under that of the imported cement, and a lessened price would extend its use in all building operations, as it is, when properly applied, better suited for this climate than the ordinary mortar.

At present I am not aware of any Nova Scotia cements in the market ; the Portlant Cement being generally called for in contracts and specifications. Among Nova Scotia limestones possessing hydraulicity may be mentioned those from Horton, Windsor, St. Peter's, Chester, Onslow, Shubenacadie, Spring Hill, Whyhogomah, etc. In the lockwork of St. Peter's Canal, Portland Cement alone was used.

The quantity burnt for agricultural purposes must be very considerable ; but no returns are made of the amount thus used, and in very many parts of the Province, nature has supplied this fertiliser in abundance. The Mines Department gives the amount of limestones and ankerite quarried during the years 1874-9, at 39,327 tons, but this refers only to that used for smelting purposes, and does not include the amount extracted by individuals throughout the Province.

CHAPTER VIII.

REFRACTORY MATERIALS.— PLUMBAGO.— FIRE CLAY.—SOAPSTONE.— POTTERY CLAY.—KAOLIN.

Plumbago.—This mineral is not uncommon in the Province, although as yet no deposits have been worked. Among the localities affording it may be mentioned—Parrsborough, Salmon River, Musquodoboit, Hammonds Plains, Fifteen-Mile Stream, Boularderie Island, Gregwa Brook, and Gillis Brook, Cape Breton. These deposits are, in many cases, really highly plumbaginous shales; but were attention directed to the subject, some might be found of economic value. In Ontario and Quebec valuable deposits of this mineral occur in the Laurentian limestones, and much interesting information on their extent and nature is to be found in the Survey Reports. The Report for 1876-7 contains a valuable paper by Mr. Hoffman, on Canadian graphites, compared with those of Ceylon.

From the returns of 1878 this mineral does not seem to be mined at present in England. Formerly only the pure granular varieties were in demand, but a much more impure ore can now be utilised; and the exports of Plumbago from Canada for the year 1878-9 were 1,029 tons, valued at $3,627. Its applications are so well known that they need not be enumerated here.

Fire Clays.—Clays are essentially hydrated silicates of alumina, also holding moisture. Their plasticity, when mixed with water, depends on the presence of the water of composition, and when heated to redness, it is driven off, and they lose this property. When these clays stand a high temperature without melting or softening, they are termed refractory or fire clays. They occur in various geological formations, those of the best quality being generally obtained from the coal measures, where they usually form the beds underlying the coal seams.

The mechanical mixtures accompanying clays are silica, carbonates of lime and magnesia, pyrites, etc. They affect the heated clay in various ways, by causing unequal expansion and cracking, and by forming fusible slags. These effects depend not only on the amounts of the impurities, but also on their relative proportions, as in the case of furnace slags. Among the purer clays are those holding large proportions of pure silicious sand, as the celebrated Dinas brick clay.

Fire brick are required to stand, in some cases, high and prolonged heat, alternations of temperature, not to soften when heated, or run when in the presence of heated metallic oxides. Any one clay will seldom meet all the above requirements, and various materials are added to counteract the failing, such as sand, powdered millstone grit, clay previously burned and ground, etc. The method of making fire brick resembles that followed in the manufacture of common brick. The clay, after weathering, is carefully ground, etc., and burned for five or six days in kilns of 15 or 20 thousand. The following analyses will show the character of typical English fire clays:

	Stourbridge.	Newcastle-on-Tyne.	Dowlais.
Silica	63·30	55·50	67·12
Alumina	23·30	27·15	21·18
Potash		2·19	2·02
Soda		·44	
Lime	·73	·67	·32
Magnesia		·75	·84
Iron Protoxide	1·80	2·01	
Iron Peroxide			1·85
Water of Combin: }	10·30	10·53	4·82
Moisture }			2·29
	99·43	99·84	100·44

Chemical analyses will frequently show that a fire clay is not adapted for use; but a satisfactory decision in any case can only be arrived at by careful practical tests.

Numerous attempts have been made in this Province to find clays suitable for the manufacture of fire brick, as the value of the article imported in the raw and manufactured state during the years 1877-78, amounted to $52,233 and $35,749, and the demand is likely to increase. The following analyses will show the composition of several Nova Scotian fire clays:

	Lingan.*	Deep Seam.*	Spring Hill.*	Stewiacke.†	Coxheath, C. B.
Silica	55·20	51·15	50·47	45·611	76·260
Alumina	32·10	22·57	32·69	14·000	19·152
Iron Oxide	1·87	6·48	8·01	6·100	trace
Titannic Acid		1·75	1·88	......	......
Lime	⎫	1·27	1·85	trace	·552
Magnesia	⎬ 5·53	1·55	2·11	1·096	·170
Alkalies	⎭	2·66	1·96	......	·259
Comb'd. Water	5.30	4·23	1·03	6·550	4·300
Moisture		2·88	....	1·000	......
Carbonic Acid		5·04	....	......	......
Organic matter		1·16	....—	......	......
Sand		....	....	25·689	......

The fire clay from Coxheath Hills, Cape Breton, is an altered felsite, compact, lustre pearly to dull, color pearl grey, greasy to the touch. The analyst, Mr. Hoffman, G. S. R., 1875-6, gives the results of numerous experiments, from which it appeared that the rock alone would not make a brick, as after burning the mass remained friable. When from half to one per cent. of lime was added an excellent refractory brick was produced. Large quantities of this rock, which is well worth a practical test, are reported by Mr. Fletcher to be exposed at Watson's Brook, and several localities in the Coxheath and East Bay Hills, as Big Pond, Gillis and Forks Lake brooks.

During 1879, a few tons of fire clay were burnt into good brick by Mr. Cameron, of Stellarton, and are being used in the construction of Coke ovens, by the Halifax Company. The clay is from a bed overlying the McGregor seam, and is four feet thick where opened on the land of the Halifax Company. I understand the manager of the Londonderry Iron Works considers it well adapted for metallurgical purposes. Messrs. Mackintosh and Dewar, are now building at New Glasgow, a plant for the manufacture of fire brick from this clay. The quality of the clay is said to have proved, under severe tests made in England, to be of the very best. It is to be hoped that this enterprise will prove successful, as the demand for this article is increasing every year. Doubtless as the search is extended, other clays will be found suitable for refractory bricks, linings, etc., and in this connection the large deposits of infusorial or silicious earth found in many of our lakes, etc., may prove of value.

Refractory Stones.—There has been so little demand for such materials that scarcely any information can be given. Some of the metamorphosed

*Analyst unknown. †E. Gilpin.

Upper Silurian clay slates of Pictou County afford stones which have been successfully used for lining cupolas, boiler furnaces, etc. I have tested the fire resisting qualities of several sandstones from the Pictou coal field, but did not find them valuable. The upper coal measures may yield sandstones adapted for furnace hearths, etc.

Soapstone has been found, I am informed, in Cape Breton, near Louisburg, and at other points; but I am in possession of no details as to its quality, etc.

At the Exhibition of 1879, very handsome samples of pottery, vases, jars, ornaments, besides tiles, drain pipes, dishes, etc., were shown by Smith & Kaye, Hornsby & Flavin, Messrs. Harrison, and others. From these the adaptability of the various white and red clays to the potter's art, was satisfactorily shown. Some years ago, pottery was made near New Glasgow, from a coal measure clay, but work has been discontinued.

Kaolin has been found in small beds, at several places on the Atlantic coast, resulting probably from the decomposition of feldspar. As yet, however, it has not received any attention. In Cornwall, a large business is carried on in this material, some of which is worked into porcelain, etc., on the spot, and the rest taken to the midland counties. The returns for 1878 give, under the Metalliferous Mines Act, 60,261 tons of potters' and other clays.

CHAPTER IX.

MATERIALS FOR GRINDING AND POLISHING.—INFUSORIAL EARTH.—GRIND-STONES.—MILLSTONES.—WHETSTONES.

Infusorial Earths.—The deposits of this material at present known are found chiefly in the lakes of the Atlantic coast, and in some bogs and swamps, which have resulted apparently from the filling up or drainage of similar waters. Wentworth, Country Harbor, St. Anns, Grand Lake, Lochaber, French River, Earltown and Cornwallis may be mentioned as localities yielding it. Beds of it are found 8 feet thick in the lakes supplying Halifax with water.* It is employed for polishing, etc., and the silicious varieties may be found useful in the manufacture of fire and bath bricks.

Grindstones.—At several points in the Province stones are found admirably adapted for the above purpose. Among the best known localities may be mentioned the Joggins, Pugwash, Glenville and Pudsely's Point, where the stones are taken from a reef, uncovered at low water, having a thickness of 20 to 30 feet. At Port Philip, both red and gray grindstones are made of all sizes, up to seven feet in diameter. Several cargoes have been shipped from Merigomish, and stones are cut for local use at several points in Cape Breton.

Granite is the material generally used here for the manufacture of millstones, and for convenience they are cut usually from the boulders found everywhere in the Province. In Ontario the stone used for this purpose is a brown cellular chert, having irregular cells, varying in diameter from a sixteenth to three-quarters of an inch. The deposit occurs filling vein-like fissures in Laurentian Syenite, and is supposed to have been deposited by water. Whetstones are made from sandstones having an argillaceous cement, frequently micaceous, at numerous points

' Prof. Lawson, N. S. Institute Natural Science, January, 1880.

n the Province, as the Joggins, Parrsboro, Colchester County, Merigomish, etc. The census of 1871 returned 3 grindstone factories in Nova Scotia, giving employment to 118 persons, with an annual product valued at $37,442.

Our chief exports of grindstones and scythe-stones are from the Joggins. Small quantities are also sent from Parrsboro, Merigomish, etc. The returns of the Mines Department give the exports of grindstones for the years 1875-76-77 and 79—(returns for 1879 not made up)—at $99,660, and of scythestones for the same years at $8,894.

CHAPTER X.

PRECIOUS STONES.—TRAP MINERALS.

Precious Stones.-Our list of precious stones for the purpose of ornament, etc., is a very limited one. A specimen of Topaz was shown at the London Exhibition of 1872, said to have come from Cape Breton. This may have been a yellow corrundum. Garnets are very common in the more highly metamorphosed slates of the gold districts. They vary in size from a pin's head to crystals one half an inch in diameter, but, I believe, are generally found to be too brittle for the purpose of the jeweller. Crystals of quartz, commonly known as rock crystals, are very common in the older rocks, and are met in great beauty in some of the gold leads. The mineral, however, is so abundant that they would be valuable only if there were a home demand to admit of their being worked here.

Amethyst, purple quartz, is a very common mineral in the trap districts, where it occurs as crystals and incrustations often of considerable size. Its value depends entirely on its depth and uniformity of color. Specimens from Nova Scotia have been much admired in England and on the continent. The early French settlers sent considerable quantities home, and one very handsome specimen was divided in two, and placed in the crown of one of the French Kings. Among localities yielding it, may be mentioned Parrsboro, Digby Neck, Cape Sharp, Blomedon, Cornwallis, Sandy Cove, etc. Smoky quartz, cairn gorm stone, is very abundant at Paradise, Annapolis County, and many of our auriferous veins present varieties of it. Heliotrope, Jasper, Chalcedony, Agate and Common Opal, are also frequently met in the trap districts. The Heliotrope, or blood-stone, finds a ready sale when in good specimens.

The trap of the Bay of Fundy has acquired an almost world wide reputation for the variety and beauty of its minerals, which have been formed by the dissolving and concentrating agency of water acting through long ages.

Dr. Gesner, the late Dr. How, and others, devoted much time to the determination and collection of these minerals, and very beautiful cabinets have been exhibited at various times. It would be foreign to the aims of this report to describe, even in the briefest terms, the various minerals and their localities, as they possess scarcely any economic value at present. The following list embraces those best known:—
Albin, Analcime, Anatase, Apatite, Apophyllite, Calcspar, Centrallasite, Cerinite, Chabazite, Chlorophœite, Chlorite, Cyanolite, Faroelite, Green Earth, Green Calcspar, Gyrolite, Heulandite, Laumonite, Lederite, Mesolite, Mordenite, Moss Agate, Natrolite, Obsidian, Phrenite, Poonah Earth, Scholesite, Sinter, Stilbite, Tremolite, Thomsonite and Wichtesite. Those who desire further information on the subject of these trap minerals, the identification, physical characteristics, etc., of their varieties, will find Dana's Mineralogy the best text book.

CHAPTER XI.

MINERALS OF THE LAURENTIAN STRATA.—TENURE OF MINERAL LANDS.—
UNITED STATES MINERAL TARIFF.

I venture to draw your attention to a series of measures which may be found to hold valuable minerals in Nova Scotia. Under the term Laurentian, or, according to the new nomenclature of the Survey, Huronian, are included a great mass of rocks, comprising reddish orthoclase gneiss, quartzite, crystalline limestones, dolomites, etc. These measures stretch from the Labrador far into Canada, and also occur in Cape Breton and Nova Scotia. With these rocks are associated in Quebec and Ontario five important minerals—Hematite, Magnetite, Apatite (phosphate of lime), Mica and Graphite. The more important deposits of Canadian iron ores are found in these measures, as beds and lenticular interstratified masses often of large size. Many of the ores are of great purity, and hold very small per-centages of sulphur and phosphorus. At various times large quantities of these ores have been exported to the United States. Of late years the export has greatly decreased, but is reviving again. The amount exported during 1878-79 was 3,562 tons, valued at $7,530.

Apatite.—This mineral, which forms the basis of the soluble superphosphates, used extensively for manure in England, promises to form a valuable adjunct to the mining and manufacturing resources of Canada. It occurs in veins in the limestones and associated strata, frequently crystalised, also compact and granular. Its color varies from green to yellow, with blue and reddish hues, with resinous to oily lustre. Its hardness is 5, or readily scratched by quartz, and it is brittle. This apatite contains usually a high per-centage of phosphate of lime, and is, with proper treatment, well adapted for making concentrated superphosphate. The Canadian mineral contains $4\frac{1}{2}$ to 7 per cent. of fluoride of calcium, which, during the usual treatment, yields hydrofluoric acid, which injures the health of the workmen employed. This objection, however, has been obviated by new processes, and Canadian, Norwegian, Spanish and Nassau phosphates can now be treated without inconvenience. The mineral has been generally shipped in lumps, but should be ground and barrelled, which facilitates handling and sampling. The amount exported during the year 1878-9 was 11,927 tons, valued at $216,295.

The appearances and uses of mica and graphite are so well known that I need not take up your time by a description of their physical properties. The G. S. Report 1876-7 contains a valuable paper by Mr. Hoffman, comparing the Canadian graphite with that exported from Ceylon. His experiments show that the Canadian graphite is as pure as that from Ceylon, and equally adapted for crucibles, etc.

The graphite occurs in the form of scales, disseminated in limestones and gneisses, or in veins cutting these rocks. Rocks containing as low as 2·4 per-centage of graphite can be treated by stamping, buddles, etc., to yield a marketable product. The folliated variety, however, is found to be purest. Considerable quantities have been mined and manufactured in Ontario. The mica occurs frequently as crystals in the limestones, usually near interstratified masses of pyroxenic gneiss, etc., and plates have been cut 20 by 30 inches.

The labors of the Geological Survey have already shown the presence in this Province of considerable areas of this series of rocks, and it appears probable that their extent will be found larger than at present is currently believed to be the case. The similarity of the strata over so wide an area, as dwelt upon in these reports, leads to the hope that they may here be also characterised by the valuable minerals referred to above. This view is supported by the discoveries of valuable ores of hematite, already alluded to.

TENURE OF MINERAL LANDS.

The grants of land to the early settlers in this Province, contained no regular reservation of minerals; in some instances, gold, silver and precious stones alone were reserved, in other cases the gold, silver coal, iron, copper, lead, etc., were retained for a source of revenue to the Crown. After the agreement, with the General Mining Association, the Government passed an act, by which they retained in previous grants, the gold, silver, copper, iron, lead, tin, coal and precious stones whenever mentioned, and made the above reservations in all future grants for the purpose of revenue. This act releases to the owner of the land, all minerals not mentioned above, such as limestones, gypsum, fire clay, barytes, manganese, etc., and any of the above reservations whenever they are not specified in the grant. There is no complete list published of the various grants, but full information as to the position, date and reservation of every grant, can be obtained from the Crown Land Office. The Department of Public Works and Mines is entrusted with the collection of the revenue from the Mines; and all leases are issued by it, etc. Gold areas are obtainable for three months as prospecting licenses, and as leases for twenty-one years, with the right of renewal. The cost of the license, which must not exceed one hundred acres in extent, is at the rate of 50 cents per acre, up to ten acres, and 25 cents for each additional acre. The lease will cost two dollars for each lot measuring 250 by 150 feet. Mill licenses are issued, and the regulations are all framed with a view of facilitating the operations of the miner. Licenses to search, covering 5 square miles of ground, and lasting one year, are issued for other minerals, at a cost of $20; and leases can be procured for a term of twenty years, renewable on complying with the requirements of the law of Mines and Minerals.

The following are the royalties paid by these holding property under lease from the Government. Nine cents and seven tenths of a cent on every ton (2,240 ℔s) of coal coarse enough not to pass the interstices of a screen having its bars ¾ of an inch apart, the fine coal and that used for colliery workmen and engines being free; three cents on every ton (2,000 ℔s.) of iron ore; ten cents on every ton (2,000 ℔s.) of copper ore, and five per cent. on the value of all other ores and minerals, except gold, which pays a royalty of two per cent., at the rate of $19 an ounce, Troy, for smelted gold, and $18.50 an ounce, Troy, for unsmelted gold. Full information on all points connected with this subject, will be found in the law of Mines and Minerals.

All the regulations connected with the leasing and working of the Provincial Mines are framed with the view of affording all proper and necessary facilities to those desirous of entering into mining operations, and among not the least of these advantages may be mentioned the absolute security of the titles, granted and registered by the Government.

The following extracts from the United States Tariff will interest those engaged in the extraction of Provincial minerals, etc.:

    Antimony Crude......................10 p. c. ad. val.
      "   Ore...............................Free
    Asbestos, manufactured................20 p. c. ad. val.
      "   Ore...............................Free

www.ingramcontent.com/pod-product-compliance
Lightning Source LLC
Chambersburg PA
CBHW020105170426
43199CB00009B/400